HE CHOSE THE NAILS

WHAT GOD DID TO WIN YOUR HEART

Max Lucado

WORD PUBLISHING
NASHVILLE
A Thomas Nelson Company

HE CHOSE THE NAILS

Library of Congress Cataloging-in-Publication Data

Lucado, Max.
He chose the nails / by Max Lucado.
p. cm.
Includes bibliographical references.
ISBN 0-8499-1655-0 (hardcover)
1. Christian life. 2. Jesus Christ—Person and offices. I. Title.

BV4501.2 .L815 2000
232—dc21 00-032517
CIP

Printed in the United States of America
01 02 03 04 05 BVG 9 8

To Jesus Christ,
Because you chose the nails

Contents

Acknowledgments

I'm clapping. Since books don't have speakers, you can't hear me. But believe me, I'm offering thunderous applause and a standing ovation to:

Liz Heaney and Karen Hill, my editors. You're always good at giving me a nudge, but this time one of you got behind and pushed, and the other stood in front and pulled. This old donkey can really be dense. Thanks for getting this project up the hill.

Dr. Roy B. Zuck from Dallas Theological Seminary. Your insights were treasured.

Steve Halliday. Another book, another great study guide.

Carol Bartley and Laura Kendall. I'm grateful for your precision with the manuscript.

The Word family. I'm honored to be a member of the team.

Oak Hills Church of Christ and staff. There is no place I'd rather be on Sundays than with you.

Special thanks to Buddy Cook, Golf Club of Texas, and La Cantera Golf Academy.

Steve and Cheryl Green. The dictionary defines the word *friend,* but you demonstrate it. Thanks for all you do.

To the Russian Christian who left a cross on my desk one Sunday a few years back. His note told how his new-found faith in

Jesus led him to retrieve the nails from an old abandoned Russian church. He formed the nails into a cross. Around the cross he wove a crown of barbed wire. This striking piece hangs on my office wall—and it also appears on the cover of this book. My gratitude goes to the one whose name I do not know, but whose heart I do.

My daughters, Jenna, Andrea, and Sara. You've been doubly patient with the writing of this book. Thanks! I'll be home early tonight.

My wife, Denalyn. My love for you will end on the same day God's love for you does.

You, the reader. If the scribblings of this author reveal a truth about the true Author, both of our efforts are worthwhile.

And to you, Jesus, we all stand and offer the loudest applause. It is one thing to write and read this story. It would be another to live it. And you did.

Long ago, even before he made the world,
God loved us and chose us in Christ to be holy
and without fault in his eyes.
His unchanging plan has always been to adopt us into
his own family by bringing us to himself through Jesus Christ.
And this gave him great pleasure.
So we praise God for the wonderful kindness he has poured
out on us because we belong to his dearly loved Son.
He is so rich in kindness that he purchased our freedom
through the blood of his Son,
and our sins are forgiven. . . .
God's secret plan has now been revealed to us;
it is a plan centered on Christ,
designed long ago according to his good pleasure.
And this is his plan:
At the right time he will bring everything together
under the authority of Christ—everything in heaven and on earth.
Furthermore, because of Christ,
we have received an inheritance from God,
for he chose us from the beginning,
and all things happen just as he decided long ago.

EPHESIANS 1:4–7, 9–11 NLT

1

YOU DID THIS FOR ME?

The gift of God is eternal life in Christ Jesus our Lord.

ROMANS 6:23 NIV

Thanks be to God for his indescribable gift!

2 CORINTHIANS 9:15 NIV

And God has reserved for his children the priceless
gift of eternal life; it is kept in heaven for you,
pure and undefiled, beyond the reach of change and decay.
And God, in his mighty power,
will make sure that you get there
safely to receive it, because you are trusting him.
It will be yours in that coming last day for all to see.

1 PETER 1:4–5 TLB

Every good and perfect gift is from above,
coming down from the Father of the heavenly lights,
who does not change like shifting shadows.
He chose to give us birth through the word of truth,
that we might be a kind of firstfruits of all he created.

JAMES 1:17–18 NIV

He deserves our compassion. When you see him, do not laugh. Do not mock. Do not turn away or shake your head. Just gently lead him to the nearest bench and help him sit down.

Have pity on the man. He is so fearful, so wide-eyed. He's a deer on the streets of Manhattan. Tarzan walking through the urban jungle. He's a beached whale, wondering how he got here and how he'll get out.

Who is this forlorn creature? This ashen-faced orphan? He is—please remove your hats out of respect—he is the man in the women's department. Looking for a gift.

The season may be Christmas. The occasion may be her birthday or their anniversary. Whatever the motive, he has come out of hiding. Leaving behind his familiar habitat of sporting goods stores, food courts, and the big-screen television in the appliance department, he ventures into the unknown world of women's wear. You'll spot him easily. He's the motionless one in the aisle. Were it not for the sweat rings under his arms, you'd think he was a mannequin.

But he isn't. He is a man in a woman's world, and he's never seen so much underwear. At the Wal-Mart where he buys his, it's all wrapped up and fits on one shelf. But here he is in a forest of lace. His father warned him about places like this. Though the sign above says "linger-ie," he knows he shouldn't.

So he moves on, but he doesn't know where to go. You see, not every man has been prepared for this moment as I was. My father saw the challenge of shopping for women as a rite of passage, right in there with birds and bees and tying neckties. He taught my brother and me how to survive when we shopped. I can remember the day he sat us down and taught us two words. To get around in a foreign country, you need to know the language, and my father taught us the language of the ladies' department.

"There will come a time," he said solemnly, "when a salesperson will offer to help you. At that moment take a deep breath and say this phrase, '*Es-tée Lau-der.*'" On every gift-giving occasion for years after, my mom received three gifts from the three men in her life: Estée Lauder, Estée Lauder, and Estée Lauder.

My fear of the women's department was gone. But then I met Denalyn. Denalyn doesn't like Estée Lauder. Though I told her it made her smell motherly, she didn't change her mind. I've been in a bind ever since.

This year for her birthday I opted to buy her a dress. When the salesperson asked me Denalyn's size, I said I didn't know. I honestly don't. I know I can wrap my arm around her and that her hand fits nicely in mine. But her dress size? I never inquired. There are certain questions a man doesn't ask.

The woman tried to be helpful. "How does she compare to me?" Now, I was taught to be polite to women, but I couldn't be polite and answer that question. There was only one answer, "She is thinner."

I stared at my feet, looking for a reply. After all, I write books. Surely I could think of the right words.

I considered being direct: "She is less of you."

Or complimentary: "You are more of a woman than she is."

Perhaps a hint would suffice? "I hear the store is *downsizing*."

Finally I swallowed and said the only thing I knew to say, "Estée Lauder?"

She pointed me in the direction of the perfume department, but I knew better than to enter. I would try the purses. Thought it would be easy. What could be complicated about selecting a tool for holding cards and money? I've used the same money clip for eight years. What would be difficult about buying a purse?

Oh, naive soul that I am. Tell an attendant in the men's department that you want a wallet, and you're taken to a small counter next to the cash register. Your only decision is black or brown. Tell an attendant in the ladies' department that you want a purse, and you are escorted to a room. A room of shelves. Shelves with purses. Purses with price tags. Small but potent price tags . . . prices so potent they should remove the need for a purse, right?

I was pondering this thought when the salesperson asked me some questions. Questions for which I had no answer. "What kind of purse would your wife like?" My blank look told her I was clueless, so she began listing the options: "Handbag? Shoulder bag? Glove bag? Backpack? Shoulder pack? Change purse?"

Dizzied by the options, I had to sit down and put my head between my knees lest I faint. Didn't stop her. Leaning over me, she continued, "Moneybag? Tote bag? Pocketbook? Satchel?"

"Satchel?" I perked up at the sound of a familiar word. Satchel Paige pitched in the major leagues. This must be the answer. I straightened my shoulders and said proudly, "Satchel."

Apparently she didn't like my answer. She began to curse at me in a foreign language. Forgive me for relating her vulgarity, but she was very crude. I didn't understand all she said, but I do know she called me a "Dooney Bird" and threatened to "brighten" me with a spade that belonged to someone named Kate. When she laid claim to "our mawny," I put my hand over the wallet in my hip pocket and defied, "No, it's my money." That was enough. I got out of there as fast as I could. But as I left the room, I gave her a bit of her own medicine. "Estée Lauder!" I shouted and ran as fast as I could.

Oh, the things we do to give gifts to those we love.

But we don't mind, do we? We would do it all again. Fact is, we *do* it all again. Every Christmas, every birthday, every so often we find ourselves in foreign territory. Grownups are in toy stores. Dads are in teen stores. Wives are in the hunting department, and husbands are in the purse department.

Not only do we enter unusual places, we do unusual things. We assemble bicycles at midnight. We hide the new tires with mag wheels under the stairs. One fellow I heard about rented a movie theater so he and his wife could see their wedding pictures on their anniversary.

And we'd do it all again. Having pressed the grapes of service, we drink life's sweetest wine—the wine of giving. We are at our best when we are giving. In fact, we are most like God when we are giving.

Have you ever wondered why God gives so much? We could

exist on far less. He could have left the world flat and gray; we wouldn't have known the difference. But he didn't.

He splashed orange in the sunrise
and cast the sky in blue.
And if you love to see geese as they gather,
chances are you'll see that too.

Did he have to make the squirrel's tail furry?
Was he obliged to make the birds sing?
And the funny way that chickens scurry
or the majesty of thunder when it rings?

Why give a flower fragrance? Why give food its taste?
Could it be
he loves to see
that look upon your face?

If we give gifts to show our love, how much more would he? If we—speckled with foibles and greed—love to give gifts, how much more does God, pure and perfect God, enjoy giving gifts to us? Jesus asked, "If you hardhearted, sinful men know how to give good gifts to your children, won't your Father in heaven even more certainly give good gifts to those who ask him for them?" (Matt. 7:11 TLB).

God's gifts shed light on God's heart, God's good and generous heart. Jesus' brother James tells us: "Every desirable and beneficial gift comes out of heaven. The gifts are rivers of light cascading down from the Father of Light" (James 1:17 MSG). Every gift reveals God's love . . . but no gift reveals his love more than the gifts of the cross. They came, not wrapped in paper, but in passion. Not placed around a tree, but a cross. And not covered with ribbons, but sprinkled with blood.

The gifts of the cross.

Much has been said about the gift of the cross itself, but what of the other gifts? What of the nails, the crown of thorns? The garments taken by the soldiers. The garments given for the burial. Have you taken time to open these gifts?

He didn't have to give them, you know. The only act, the only *required* act for our salvation was the shedding of blood, yet he did much more. So much more. Search the scene of the cross, and what do you find?

A wine-soaked sponge.

A sign.

Two crosses beside Christ.

Divine gifts intended to stir that moment, that split second when your face will brighten, your eyes will widen, and God will hear you whisper, "You did this for me?"

The diadem of pain
which sliced your gentle face,
three spikes piercing flesh and wood
to hold you in your place.

The need for blood I understand.
Your sacrifice I embrace.
But the bitter sponge, the cutting spear,
the spit upon your face?
Did it have to be a cross?

Did not a kinder death exist
than six hours hanging between life and death,
all spurred by a betrayer's kiss?

"Oh, Father," you pose,
heart-stilled at what could be,
"I'm sorry to ask, but I long to know,
did you do this for me?"

Dare we pray such a prayer? Dare we think such thoughts? Could it be that the hill of the cross is rich with God's gifts? Let's examine them, shall we? Let's unwrap these gifts of grace as if—or perhaps, indeed—for the first time. And as you touch them—as you feel the timber of the cross and trace the braid of the crown and finger the point of the spike—pause and listen. Perchance you will hear him whisper:

"I did it just for you."

2

"I WILL BEAR YOUR DARK SIDE"

God's Promise in the Soldiers' Spit

Sin lurks deep in the hearts of the wicked,
forever urging them on to evil deeds.

PSALM 36:1 TLB

Vanity is so anchored in the heart of man that . . . those who write against it want to have the glory of having written well; and those who read it desire the glory of having read it.

BLAISE PASCAL

The heart is deceitful above all things
and beyond cure.
Who can understand it?

JEREMIAH 17:9 NIV

Sin, understood in the Christian sense, is the rent which cuts through the whole of existence.

EMIL BRUNNER

Oh this propensity to evil, how did you creep in to cover the earth with treachery?

ECCLESIASTICUS 37:3 APOC

What would have happened to the Beast if the Beauty hadn't appeared?

You know the story. There was a time when his face was handsome and his palace pleasant. But that was before the curse, before the shadows fell on the castle of the prince, before the shadows fell on the heart of the prince. And when the darkness fell, he hid. Secluded in his castle, he was left with glistening snout and curly tusks and a bad mood.

But all that changed when the girl came. I wonder, what would have happened to the Beast if the Beauty hadn't appeared?

Better yet, what would have happened if she hadn't cared? Who would have blamed her if she hadn't? He was such a . . . well, such a beast. Hairy. Drooling. Roaring. Defying. And she was such a beauty. Stunningly gorgeous. Contagiously kind. If ever two people lived up to their names, didn't the Beauty and the Beast? Who would have blamed her if she hadn't cared? But she did care.

And because the Beauty loved the Beast, the Beast became more beautiful himself.

The story's familiar, not just because it's a fairy tale. It's familiar because it reminds us of ourselves. There is a beast within each of us.

It wasn't always so. There was a time when humanity's face was beautiful and the palace pleasant. But that was before the curse, before the shadow fell across the garden of Adam, before the shadow fell across the heart of Adam. And ever since the curse, we've been different. Beastly. Ugly. Defiant. Angry. We do things we know we shouldn't do and wonder why we did them.

The ugly part of me sure showed his beastly face the other night. I was driving on a two-lane road that was about to become a single lane. A woman in a car beside me was in the lane that continued. I was in the one that stopped. I needed to be ahead of her. My schedule was, no doubt, more important than hers. After all, am I not a man of the cloth? Am I not a courier of compassion? An ambassador of peace?

So I floored it.

Guess what? She did, too. When my lane ended, she was a fender ahead of me. I growled and slowed and let her go ahead. Over her shoulder she gave me a sweet little bye-bye wave. Grrrr.

I started to dim my headlights. Then I paused. The sinister part of me said, "Wait a minute." Am I not called to shed light on dark places? Illuminate the shadows?

So I put a little high beam in her rearview mirror.

She retaliated by slowing down. To a crawl. This woman was mean. She couldn't have cared less if the whole city of San Antonio was late; she wasn't going to go beyond fifteen miles per hour. And I wasn't going to take my lights out of her rearview mirror. Like two stubborn donkeys, she kept it slow and I kept it bright. After more unkind thoughts than I dare confess, the road widened and I started to pass. Wouldn't you know it? A red light left the two of us side by side at an intersection. What happened next contains both good news and bad. The good news is, she waved at me. The bad news is, her wave was not one you'd want to imitate.

Moments later, conviction surfaced. "Why did I do that?" I'm typically a calm guy, but for fifteen minutes I was a beast! Only two facts comforted me: One, I don't have a fish symbol on my car, and two, the apostle Paul had similar struggles. "I do not do what I want to do, and I do the things I hate" (Rom. 7:15). Ever felt like saying those words?

If so, you're in good company. Paul isn't the only person in the Bible who wrestled the beast within. Hard to find a page in Scripture where the animal doesn't bare his teeth. King Saul chasing young David with a spear. Shechem raping Dinah. Dinah's brothers (the sons of Jacob) murdering Shechem and his friends. Lot selling out to Sodom and then getting out of Sodom. Herod murdering Bethlehem toddlers. Another Herod murdering Jesus' cousin. If the Bible is called the Good Book, it's not because its people are. Blood runs as freely through the stories as the ink through the quills that penned them. But the evil of the beast was never so raw as on the day Christ died.

The disciples were first fast asleep, then fast afoot.

Herod wanted a show.

Pilate wanted out.

And the soldiers? They wanted blood.

So they scourged Jesus. The legionnaire's whip consisted of leather straps with lead balls on each end. His goal was singular:

Beat the accused within an inch of his death and then stop. Thirty-nine lashes were allowed but seldom needed. A centurion monitored the prisoner's status. No doubt Jesus was near death when his hands were untied and he slumped to the ground.

The whipping was the first deed of the soldiers.

The crucifixion was the third. (No, I didn't skip the second. We'll get to that in a moment.) Though his back was ribboned with wounds, the soldiers loaded the crossbeam on Jesus' shoulders and marched him to the Place of a Skull and executed him.

We don't fault the soldiers for these two actions. After all, they were just following orders. But what's hard to understand is what they did in between. Here is Matthew's description:

> Jesus was beaten with whips and handed over to the soldiers to be crucified. The governor's soldiers took Jesus into the governor's palace, and they all gathered around him. They took off his clothes and put a red robe on him. Using thorny branches, they made a crown, put it on his head, and put a stick in his right hand. Then the soldiers bowed before Jesus and made fun of him, saying, "Hail, King of the Jews!" They spat on Jesus. Then they took his stick and began to beat him on the head. After they finished, the soldiers took off the robe and put his own clothes on him again. Then they led him away to be crucified. (Matt. 27:26–31)

The soldiers' assignment was simple: Take the Nazarene to the hill and kill him. But they had another idea. They wanted to have some fun first. Strong, rested, armed soldiers encircled an exhausted, nearly dead, Galilean carpenter and beat up on him. The scourging was commanded. The crucifixion was ordered. But who would draw pleasure out of spitting on a half-dead man?

Spitting isn't intended to hurt the body—it can't. Spitting is intended to degrade the soul, and it does. What were the soldiers doing? Were they not elevating themselves at the expense of another? They felt big by making Christ look small.

Ever done that? Maybe you've never spit on anyone, but have you gossiped? Slandered? Have you ever raised your hand in anger or rolled your eyes in arrogance? Have you ever blasted your high beams in someone's rearview mirror? Ever made someone feel bad so you would feel good?

That's what the soldiers did to Jesus. When you and I do the same, we do it to Jesus too. "I assure you, when you did it to one of the least of these my brothers and sisters, you were doing it to me!" (Matt. 25:40 NLT). How we treat others is how we treat Jesus.

"Oh, Max, I don't like to hear that," you protest. Believe me, I don't like to say it. But we must face the fact that there is something beastly within each and every one of us. Something beastly that makes us do things that surprise even us. Haven't you surprised yourself? Haven't you reflected on an act and wondered, "What got into me?"

The Bible has a three-letter answer for that question: S-I-N. There is something bad—beastly—within each of us. We are "by nature children of wrath" (Eph. 2:3 NASB). It is not that we *can't* do good. We do. It's just that we can't keep from doing bad. In theological terms, we are "totally depraved." Though made in God's image, we have fallen. We're corrupt at the core. The very center of our being is selfish and perverse. David said, "I was born a sinner—yes, from the moment my mother conceived me" (Ps. 51:5 NLT). Could any of us say any less? Each one of us was born with a tendency to sin. Depravity is a universal condition. Scripture says it plainly:

> All we like sheep have gone astray; we have turned, every one, to his own way. (Isa. 53:6 NKJV)
>
> The heart is deceitful above all things and beyond cure. Who can understand it? (Jer. 17:9 NIV)
>
> There is none righteous, no, not one. . . . All have sinned and fall short of the glory of God. (Rom. 3:10, 23 NKJV)

Some would disagree with such strong words. They look around and say, "Compared to everyone else, I'm a decent person." You know, a pig might say something similar. He might look at his trough partners and announce, "I'm just as clean as everyone else." Compared to humans, however, that pig needs help. Compared to God, we humans need the same. The standard for sinlessness isn't found at the pig troughs of earth but at the throne of heaven. God, himself, is the standard.

We are beasts. As French essayist Michel de Montaigne said, "There is no man so good, who, were he to submit all his thoughts and actions to the laws, would not deserve hanging ten times in his life."[1] Our deeds are ugly. Our actions are harsh. We don't do what we want to do, we don't like what we do, and what's worse—yes, there is something worse—we can't change.

We try, oh, how we try. But "Can a leopard change his spots? In the same way, Jerusalem, you cannot change and do good, because you are accustomed to doing evil" (Jer. 13:23). The apostle agreed with the prophet: "The mind that is set on the flesh is hostile to God; it does not submit to God's law—*indeed it cannot"* (Rom. 8:7 NRSV, emphasis mine).

Still disagree? Still think the assessment is too harsh? If so, accept this challenge. For the next twenty-four hours lead a sinless life. I'm not asking for a perfect decade or year or even a perfect month. Just one perfect day. Can you do it? Can you live without sin for one day?

No? How about one hour? Could you promise that for the next sixty minutes you will have only pure thoughts and actions?

Still hesitant? Then how about the next five minutes? Five minutes of worry-free, anger-free, unselfish living—can you do it?

No? Nor can I.

Then we have a problem: We are sinners, and "the wages of sin is death" (Rom. 6:23 NIV).

We have a problem: We are not holy, and "anyone whose life is not holy will never see the Lord" (Heb. 12:14).

We have a problem: We are evil, and "evil people are paid with punishment" (Prov. 10:16).

What can we do?

Allow the spit of the soldiers to symbolize the filth in our hearts. And then observe what Jesus does with our filth. He carries it to the cross.

Through the prophet he said, "I did not hide my face from mocking and spitting" (Isa. 50:6 NIV). Mingled with his blood and sweat was the essence of our sin.

God could have deemed otherwise. In God's plan, Jesus was offered wine for his throat, so why not a towel for his face? Simon carried the cross of Jesus, but he didn't mop the cheek of Jesus. Angels were a prayer away. Couldn't they have taken the spittle away?

They could have, but Jesus never commanded them to. For some reason, the One who chose the nails also chose the saliva. Along with the spear and the sponge of man, he bore the spit of man. Why? Could it be that he sees the beauty within the beast?

But here the correlation with *Beauty and the Beast* ends. In the fable, the beauty kisses the beast. In the Bible, the Beauty does much more. He becomes the beast so the beast can become the beauty. Jesus changes places with us. We, like Adam, were under a curse, but Jesus "changed places with us and put himself under that curse" (Gal. 3:13).

What if the Beauty had not come? What if the Beauty had not cared? Then we would have remained a beast. But the Beauty did come, and the Beauty did care.

The sinless One took on the face of a sinner so that we sinners could take on the face of a saint.

3

"I LOVED YOU ENOUGH TO BECOME ONE OF YOU"

God's Promise in the Crown of Thorns

God was pleased for all of himself to live in Christ.

COLOSSIANS 1:19

The Word became flesh and made his
dwelling among us. We have seen his glory,
the glory of the One and Only, who came from the Father,
full of grace and truth.

JOHN 1:14 NIV

I and the Father are one.

JOHN 10:30 NIV

You were bought, not with something that ruins like gold or silver,
but with the precious blood of Christ,
who was like a pure and perfect lamb.
Christ was chosen before the world was made,
but he was shown to the world in these last times for your sake.

1 PETER 1:18–20

He not only perfectly understands our case and our problem,
but He has morally, actively, finally solved it.

P. T. FORSYTH

You know the coolest thing about the coming of Christ? You know the most remarkable part of the incarnation?

Not just that he swapped eternity for calendars. Though such an exchange deserves our notice.

Scripture says that the number of God's years is unsearchable (Job 36:26). We may search out the moment the first wave slapped on a shore or the first star burst in the sky, but we'll never find the first moment when God was God, for there is no moment when God was not God. He has never *not been,* for he is eternal. God is not bound by time.

But when Jesus came to the earth, all this changed. He heard for the first time a phrase never used in heaven: "Your time is up." As a child, he had to leave the Temple because his time was up. As a man, he had to leave Nazareth because his time was up. And as a Savior, he had to die because his time was up. For thirty-three years, the stallion of heaven lived in the corral of time.

That's certainly remarkable, but there is something even more so.

You want to see the brightest jewel in the treasure of incarnation? You might think it was the fact that he lived in a body. One moment he was a boundless spirit; the next he was flesh and bones. Remember these words of King David? "Where can I go to get away from your Spirit? Where can I run from you? If I go up to the heavens, you are there. If I lie down in the grave, you are there. If I rise with the sun in the east and settle in the west beyond the sea, even there you would guide me" (Ps. 139:7–10).

Our asking "Where is God?" is like a fish asking "Where is water?" or a bird asking "Where is air?" God is everywhere! Equally present in Peking and Peoria. As active in the lives of Icelanders as in the lives of Texans. The dominion of God is "from sea to sea and from the River to the ends of the earth" (Ps. 72:8 NIV). We cannot find a place where God is not.

Yet when God entered time and became a man, he who was boundless became bound. Imprisoned in flesh. Restricted by weary-prone muscles and eyelids. For more than three decades, his once limitless reach would be limited to the stretch of an arm, his speed checked to the pace of human feet.

I wonder, was he ever tempted to reclaim his boundlessness? In the middle of a long trip, did he ever consider transporting himself to the next city? When the rain chilled his bones, was he tempted to change the weather? When the heat parched his lips, did he give thought to popping over to the Caribbean for some refreshment?

If ever he entertained such thoughts, he never gave in to them. Not once. Stop and think about this. Not once did Christ use his supernatural powers for personal comfort. With one word he could've transformed the hard earth into a soft bed, but he didn't.

With a wave of his hand, he could've boomeranged the spit of his accusers back into their faces, but he didn't. With an arch of his brow, he could've paralyzed the hand of the soldier as he braided the crown of thorns. But he didn't.

Remarkable. But is this the most remarkable part of the coming? Many would argue not. Many, perhaps most, would point beyond the surrender of timelessness and boundlessness to the surrender of sinlessness. It's easy to see why.

Isn't this the message of the crown of thorns?

An unnamed soldier took branches—mature enough to bear thorns, nimble enough to bend—and wove them into a crown of mockery, a crown of thorns.

Throughout Scripture thorns symbolize, not sin, but the consequence of sin. Remember Eden? After Adam and Eve sinned, God cursed the land: "So I will put a curse on the ground. . . . The ground will produce thorns and weeds for you, and you will eat the plants of the field" (Gen. 3:17–18). Brambles on the earth are the product of sin in the heart.

This truth is echoed in God's words to Moses. He urged the Israelites to purge the land of godless people. Disobedience would result in difficulties. "But if you don't force those people out of the land, they will bring you trouble. They will be like sharp hooks in your eyes and thorns in your sides" (Num. 33:55).

Rebellion results in thorns. "Evil people's lives are like paths covered with thorns and traps" (Prov. 22:5). Jesus even compared the lives of evil people to a thornbush. In speaking of false prophets, he said, "You will know these people by what they do. Grapes don't come from thornbushes, and figs don't come from thorny weeds" (Matt. 7:16).

The fruit of sin is thorns—spiny, prickly, cutting thorns.

I emphasize the "point" of the thorns to suggest a point you may have never considered: If the fruit of sin is thorns, isn't the thorny crown on Christ's brow a picture of the fruit of our sin that pierced his heart?

What is the fruit of sin? Step into the briar patch of humanity and feel a few thistles. Shame. Fear. Disgrace. Discouragement. Anxiety. Haven't our hearts been caught in these brambles?

The heart of Jesus, however, had not. He had never been cut by the thorns of sin. What you and I face daily, he never knew. Anxiety? He never worried! Guilt? He was never guilty! Fear? He never left the presence of God! Jesus never knew the fruits of sin . . . until he became sin for us.

And when he did, all the emotions of sin tumbled in on him like shadows in a forest. He felt anxious, guilty, and alone. Can't you hear the emotion in his prayer? "My God, my God, why have you rejected me?" (Matt. 27:46). These are not the words of a saint. This is the cry of a sinner.

And this prayer is one of the most remarkable parts of his coming. But I can think of something even greater. Want to know what it is? Want to know the coolest thing about the coming?

Not that the One who played marbles with the stars gave it up to play marbles with marbles. Or that the One who hung the galaxies gave it up to hang doorjambs to the displeasure of a cranky client who wanted everything yesterday but couldn't pay for anything until tomorrow.

Not that he, in an instant, went from needing nothing to needing air, food, a tub of hot water and salts for his tired feet, and, more than anything, needing somebody—anybody—who was more concerned about where he would spend eternity than where he would spend Friday's paycheck.

Or that he resisted the urge to fry the two-bit, self-appointed hall monitors of holiness who dared suggest that he was doing the work of the devil.

Not that he kept his cool while the dozen best friends he ever had felt the heat and got out of the kitchen. Or that he gave no command to the angels who begged, "Just give the nod, Lord. One word and these demons will be deviled eggs."

Not that he refused to defend himself when blamed for every sin of every slut and sailor since Adam. Or that he stood silent as a million guilty verdicts echoed in the tribunal of heaven and the giver of light was left in the chill of a sinner's night.

Not even that after three days in a dark hole he stepped into the Easter sunrise with a smile and a swagger and a question for lowly Lucifer—"Is that your best punch?"

That was cool, incredibly cool.

But want to know the coolest thing about the One who gave up the crown of heaven for a crown of thorns?

He did it for you. Just for you.

4

"I FORGIVE YOU"

God's Promise in the Nails

He forgave all our sins. He canceled the debt,
which listed all the rules we failed to follow.
He took away that record with its rules and nailed it to the cross.

COLOSSIANS 2:13–14

When we say that grace is procured for us by the merit of Christ,
we intend, that we have been purified by his blood,
and that his death was an expiation for our sins.

JOHN CALVIN

There is no difference, for all have sinned and fall
short of the glory of God, and are justified freely
by his grace through the redemption that
came by Christ Jesus. God presented him as a sacrifice
of atonement, through faith in his blood.

ROMANS 3:22–25 NIV

For all at once all sin is atoned for on the Cross,
the entire Fall is erased, and the whole obligation to Satan
and the entire sentence passed upon the fall of Adam is torn up,
cancelled, and annulled by the nails of Jesus.

COUNT NIKOLAUS LUDWIG VON ZINZENDORF

He never should have asked me to keep the list. I dread showing it to him. He's a skilled builder, a fine friend. And he has built us a great house. But the house has a few mistakes.

Until this week I didn't see them. But, then again, until this week I didn't live in the house. Once you take up residence in a place, you see every flaw.

"Make a list of them," he told me.

"If you say so," I thought.

A bedroom door won't lock. The storage room window is cracked. Someone forgot to install towel racks in the girls' bathroom. Someone else forgot the knobs to the den door. As I said, the house is nice, but the list is growing.

Looking at the list of the builder's mistakes caused me to think about God making a list of mine. After all, hasn't he taken up residence in my heart? And if I see flaws in my house, imagine what he sees in me. Oh, dare we think of the list he could compile?

The door hinges to the prayer room have grown rusty from underuse.

The stove called jealousy is overheating.

The attic floor is weighted with too many regrets.

The cellar is cluttered with too many secrets.

And won't someone raise the shutter and chase the pessimism out of this heart?

The list of our weaknesses. Would you like anyone to see yours? Would you like them made public? How would you feel if they were posted high so that everyone, including Christ himself, could see?

May I take you to the moment it was? Yes, there is a list of your failures. Christ has chronicled your shortcomings. And, yes, that list has been made public. But you've never seen it. Neither have I.

Come with me to the hill of Calvary, and I'll tell you why.

Watch as the soldiers shove the Carpenter to the ground and stretch his arms against the beams. One presses a knee against a forearm and a spike against a hand. Jesus turns his face toward the nail just as the soldier lifts the hammer to strike it.

Couldn't Jesus have stopped him? With a flex of the biceps, with a clench of the fist, he could have resisted. Is this not the same hand that stilled the sea? Cleansed the Temple? Summoned the dead?

But the fist doesn't clench . . . and the moment isn't aborted.

The mallet rings and the skin rips and the blood begins to drip, then rush. Then the questions follow. Why? Why didn't Jesus resist?

"Because he loved us," we reply. That is true, wonderfully true, but—forgive me—only partially true. There is more to his reason. He saw something that made him stay. As the soldier pressed his arm, Jesus rolled his head to the side, and with his cheek resting on the wood he saw:

A mallet? Yes.

A nail? Yes.

The soldier's hand? Yes.

But he saw something else. He saw the hand of God. It appeared to be the hand of a man. Long fingers of a woodworker. Callous palms of a carpenter. It appeared common. It was, however, anything but.

These fingers formed Adam out of clay and furrowed truth into tablets.

With a wave, this hand toppled Babel's tower and split the Red Sea.

From this hand flew the locusts that plagued Egypt and the raven that fed Elijah.

Is it any wonder the psalmist celebrated liberation by declaring: "You drove out the nations with Your hand. . . . It was Your right hand, Your arm, and the light of Your countenance" (Ps. 44:2–3 NKJV).

The hand of God is a mighty hand.

Oh, the hands of Jesus. Hands of incarnation at his birth. Hands of liberation as he healed. Hands of inspiration as he taught. Hands of dedication as he served. And hands of salvation as he died.

The crowd at the cross concluded that the purpose of the pounding was to skewer the hands of Christ to a beam. But they were only half-right. We can't fault them for missing the other half. They couldn't see it. But Jesus could. And heaven could. And we can.

Through the eyes of Scripture we see what others missed but what Jesus saw. "He canceled the record that contained the charges against us. He took it and destroyed it by nailing it to Christ's cross" (Col. 2:14 NLT).

Between his hand and the wood there was a list. A long list. A list of our mistakes: our lusts and lies and greedy moments and prodigal years. A list of our sins.

Dangling from the cross is an itemized catalog of your sins. The bad decisions from last year. The bad attitudes from last week. There, in broad daylight for all of heaven to see, is a list of your mistakes.

God has done with us what I am doing with our house. He has penned a list of our faults. The list God has made, however, cannot be read. The words can't be deciphered. The mistakes are covered. The sins are hidden. Those at the top are hidden by his hand; those down the list are covered by his blood. Your sins are "blotted out" by Jesus (KJV). "He has forgiven you all your sins: he has utterly wiped out the written evidence of broken commandments which always hung over our heads, and has completely annulled it by nailing it to the cross" (Col. 2:14 PHILLIPS).

This is why he refused to close his fist. He saw the list! What kept him from resisting? This warrant, this tabulation of your failures. He knew the price of those sins was death. He knew the source of those sins was you, and since he couldn't bear the thought of eternity without you, he chose the nails.

The hand squeezing the handle was not a Roman infantryman.

The force behind the hammer was not an angry mob.

The verdict behind the death was not decided by jealous Jews.

Jesus himself chose the nails.

So the hands of Jesus opened up. Had the soldier hesitated, Jesus himself would have swung the mallet. He knew how; he was no stranger to the driving of nails. As a carpenter he knew what it took. And as a Savior he knew what it meant. He knew that the purpose of the nail was to place your sins where they could be hidden by his sacrifice and covered by his blood.

So Jesus himself swung the hammer.

The same hand that stilled the seas stills your guilt.

The same hand that cleansed the Temple cleanses your heart.

The hand is the hand of God.

The nail is the nail of God.

And as the hands of Jesus opened for the nail, the doors of heaven opened for you.

5

"I WILL SPEAK TO YOU IN YOUR LANGUAGE"

God's Promise Through the Sign

Pilate wrote a sign and put it on the cross.
It read: JESUS OF NAZARETH, THE KING OF THE JEWS.

JOHN 19:19

So faith comes from what is heard,
and what is heard comes through the word of Christ.

ROMANS 10:17 NRSV

I am certain that when I enter the pulpit to preach or
stand at the lectern to read, it is not my word,
but my tongue is the pen of a ready writer.

MARTIN LUTHER

Long before I married, I knew the importance of reading the signs of your spouse. Wise is the man who learns the nonverbal language of his wife, who notes the nod and discerns the gestures. It's not just what is said, but how. It's not just how, but when. It's not just when, but where. Good husbanding is good decoding. You've got to read the signs.

I thought I was doing a pretty good job that weekend in Miami. Just a few months into our marriage we were hosting company in our apartment. I'd invited a Sunday guest speaker to stay with us on Saturday night. Risky move on my part since this man wasn't a college chum; he was an older, distinguished professor. Not just any professor, but a specialist in family relations. Gulp! Our new family was going to host a family specialist!

When Denalyn heard the news, she gave me a sign, a verbal sign: "We better clean the apartment." On Friday night she issued a second sign, a nonverbal sign. She got down on her knees and began scrubbing the kitchen floor. Much to my credit, I put the two signs together and got the message and got off the couch.

"What can I do to help?" I thought. Never one to tackle the simple jobs, I passed on dusting and vacuuming and looked for a more challenging task. After a diligent search, I thought of the perfect one. I would fill a picture frame with pictures. One of our wedding gifts was a collage picture frame. We hadn't even unpacked it, much less filled it. But all that would change tonight.

So I got to work. With Denalyn scrubbing floors behind me and an unmade bed beside me, I dumped a shoebox of photos in front of me and started to assemble the pictures. (I don't know what I was thinking. I guess I would have told the guest, "Hey, step over the laundry on the floor and look at our photo collection.")

I had missed the message. When Denalyn, with a chill in her voice that would have frozen perdition, asked me what I was doing, I still missed the message. "Just making a collage of pictures," I replied joyfully. For the next half-hour or so, she didn't speak. No problem. I assumed she was praying, thanking God for such a thoughtful mate. I imagined her thinking, "Maybe he'll work on our scrapbook next."

But such were not her thoughts. My first clue that something was wrong was her final pronouncement of the evening. Having single-handedly cleaned the entire apartment, she announced, "I'm going to bed. I'm very upset. Tomorrow morning I will tell you why."

Duh.

Sometimes we miss the signs. (Even now some good-hearted, yet clueless male reader is wondering, "Why was she upset?" You'll learn, my friend. You'll learn.)

The framer of our destiny is familiar with our denseness. God knows we sometimes miss the signs. Maybe that's why he has given us so many. The rainbow after the flood signifies God's covenant.

Circumcision identifies God's chosen, and the stars portray the size of his family. Even today, we see signs in the New Testament church. Communion is a sign of his death, and baptism is a sign of our spiritual birth. Each of these signs symbolizes a greater spiritual truth.

The most poignant sign, however, was found on the cross. A trilingual, hand-painted, Roman-commissioned sign.

> Pilate wrote a sign and put it on the cross. It read: JESUS OF NAZARETH, THE KING OF THE JEWS. The sign was written in Hebrew, in Latin, and in Greek. Many of the people read the sign, because the place where Jesus was crucified was near the city. The leading priests said to Pilate, "Don't write, 'The King of the Jews.' But write, 'This man said, "I am the King of the Jews."'"
>
> Pilate answered, "What I have written, I have written." (John 19:19–22)

Why is a sign placed over the head of Jesus? Why does its wording trouble the Jews, and why does Pilate refuse to change it? Why are the words written in three languages, and why is the sign mentioned in all four Gospels?

Of all the possible answers to these questions, let's focus on one. Could it be that this piece of wood is a picture of God's devotion? A symbol of his passion to tell the world about his Son? A reminder that God will do whatever it takes to share with you the message of this sign? I suggest that the sign reveals two truths about God's desire to reach the world.

There is no person he will not use.

Please note that the sign bears immediate fruit. Remember the response of the criminal? Moments from his own death, in a maelstrom of pain, he turns and says, "Jesus, remember me when you come into your kingdom" (Luke 23:42).

What an interesting choice of words. He doesn't plead, "Save me." He doesn't beg, "Have mercy on my soul." His appeal is that of a servant to a king. Why? Why does he refer to Jesus' kingdom? Perhaps he had heard Jesus speak. Maybe he was acquainted with Jesus' claims. Or, more likely, he read the sign: "Jesus of Nazareth, the King of the Jews."

Luke seems to make the connection between the reading of the sign and the offering of the prayer. In one passage he writes: "At the top of the cross these words were written: THIS IS THE KING OF THE JEWS" (Luke 23:38). Four quick verses later we read the petition of the thief: "Jesus, remember me when you come into your kingdom."

The thief knows he is in a royal mess. He turns his head and reads a royal proclamation and asks for royal help. It might have been this simple. If so, the sign was the first tool used to proclaim the message of the cross. Countless others have followed, from the printing press to the radio to the stadium crusade to the book you are holding. But a crude wooden sign preceded them all. And because of the sign, a soul was saved. All because someone posted a sign on a cross.

I don't know if the angels do entrance interviews in heaven, but if they do, this one would have been fun to witness. Imagine the thief arriving at the Pearly Gates Processing Center.

ANGEL: Have a seat. Now, tell me, Mr. . . . uh . . . Thief, how did you come to be saved?

THIEF: I just asked Jesus to remember me in his kingdom. Sure didn't expect it to happen so quickly.

ANGEL: I see. And just how did you know he was a king?

THIEF: There was a sign over his head: "Jesus of Nazareth, the King of the Jews." I believed the sign and—here I am!

ANGEL: *(Taking notes on a pad)* Believed . . . a . . . sign.

THIEF: That's right. The sign was put there by some guy named John.

ANGEL: Don't think so.

THIEF: Hmmm. Maybe it was that other follower, Peter.

ANGEL: Nope, wasn't Peter.

THIEF: Then which apostle did it?

ANGEL: Well, if you really want to know, the sign was Pilate's idea.

THIEF: No kidding? Pilate, huh?

ANGEL: Don't be surprised. God used a bush to call Moses and a donkey to convict a prophet. To get Jonah's attention, God used a big fish. There is no person he won't use. Well, that about wraps it up. *(Stamps paper)* Take this to the next window. *(Thief begins to exit)* Just follow the signs.

Pilate did not intend to spread the gospel. In fact, the sign said in so many words, "This is what becomes of a Jewish king; this is what the Romans do with him. The king of this nation is a slave; a crucified criminal: and if such be the king, what must the nation be whose king he is?"[1] Pilate had intended the sign to threaten and mock the Jews. But God had another purpose . . . Pilate was God's instrument for spreading the gospel. Unknown to himself, he was the amanuensis of heaven. He took dictation from God and wrote it on a sign. And the sign changed the destiny of a reader.

There is no one God won't use.

C. S. Lewis can tell you. We wouldn't like to imagine the twentieth century without C. S. Lewis. This Oxford professor came to Christ in his adult years, and his pen has helped millions do the same. It would be hard to find a writer with wider appeal and deeper spiritual insight. And it would be hard to find a more peculiar evangelist than the one who led Lewis to Christ.

He didn't mean to, mind you, for he himself was not a believer. His name was T. D. Weldon. He, like Lewis, was agnostic. According to one biographer, he "scoffed at all creeds and almost all positive assertions." Lewis would write that Weldon "believes that he has seen through everything and lives at rock bottom." Weldon was an intellectual, cynical unbeliever. But Weldon made a comment one day that rerouted Lewis's life. He had been studying a theologian's defense of the Gospels. "Rum thing," he commented (as only a Britisher can), "that stuff of . . . the Dying God. It almost looks as if it really happened." Lewis could hardly believe what he had heard. At first he wondered if Weldon was drunk. The statement—though offhand and casual—was enough to cause Lewis to consider that Jesus might actually be who he claimed to be.[2]

A thief is led to Christ by one who rejected Christ. A scholar is led to Christ by one who didn't believe in Christ.

There is no person he will not use. And,

There is no language God will not speak.

Every passerby could read the sign, for every passerby could read Hebrew, Latin, or Greek—the three great languages of the ancient world. "Hebrew was the language of Israel, the language of religion; Latin the language of the Romans, the language of law and government; and Greek the language of Greece, the language of culture. Christ was declared king in them all."[3] God had a message for each. "Christ is king." The message was the same, but the languages were different. Since Jesus was a king for all people, the message would be in the tongues of all people.

There is no language he will not speak. Which leads us to a delightful question. What language is he speaking to you? I'm not referring to an idiom or dialect but to the day-to-day drama of your life. God does speak, you know. He speaks to us in whatever language we will understand.

There are times he speaks the "language of abundance." Is your tummy full? Are your bills paid? Got a little jingle in your pocket? Don't be so proud of what you have that you miss what you need to hear. Could it be you have much so you can give much? "God can give you more blessings than you need. Then you will always have plenty of everything—enough to give to every good work" (2 Cor. 9:8).

Is God talking in the "language of abundance"? Or are you hearing the "vernacular of want"? We'd rather he spoke the language of abundance, but he doesn't always.

May I share a time when God gave me a message using the grammar of need? The birth of our first child coincided with the cancellation of our health insurance. I still don't understand how it happened. It had to do with the company being based in the U.S. and Jenna being born in Brazil. Denalyn and I were left with the joy of an eight-pound baby girl and the burden of a twenty-five-hundred-dollar hospital bill.

We settled the bill by draining a savings account. Thankful to be able to pay the debt but bewildered by the insurance problem, I wondered, "Is God trying to tell us something?"

A few weeks later the answer came. I spoke at a retreat for a small, happy church in Florida. A member of the congregation handed me an envelope and said, "This is for your family." Such gifts were not uncommon. We were accustomed to and grateful for these unsolicited donations, which usually amounted to fifty or a hundred dollars. I expected the amount to be comparable. But when I opened the envelope, the check was for (you guessed it) twenty-five hundred dollars.

Through the language of need, God spoke to me. It was as if he said, "Max, I'm involved in your life. I will take care of you."

Are you hearing the "language of need"? Or how about the "language of affliction"? Talk about an idiom we avoid. But you and I both know how clearly God speaks in hospital hallways and sickbeds. We know what David meant with the words, "He *makes* me to lie down" (Ps. 23:2 NKJV, italics mine). Nothing seems to turn our ears toward heaven like a frail body.

God speaks all languages—including yours. Has he not said, "I will . . . teach you in the way you should go" (Ps. 32:8 NIV)? Are we not urged to "receive instruction from His mouth" (Job 22:22 NASB)? What language is God speaking to you?

And aren't you glad he is speaking? Aren't you grateful that he cares enough to talk? Isn't it good to know that "the LORD tells his secrets to those who respect him" (Ps. 25:14)?

My Uncle Carl was grateful that someone spoke to him. A

childhood case of the measles left him unable to hear or speak. Nearly all of his sixty-plus years were lived in stony silence. Few people spoke his language.

My father was one of them. Being the older brother, maybe he felt protective. After their father died, perhaps he felt he should take over. Whatever the reason, my dad learned sign language. Dad wasn't an avid student. He never finished high school. Never went to college. Never saw the need to learn Spanish or French. But he did take the time to learn the language of his brother.

Let Dad enter the room, and Carl's face would brighten. The two would find a corner, and the hands would fly, and they would have a great time. And though I never heard Carl say thanks (he couldn't), his huge smile left no doubt that he was grateful. My dad had learned his language.

Your father has learned to speak your language as well. "It has been given to you to know the mysteries of the kingdom of heaven" (Matt. 13:11 NKJV). Think a word of thanks to him would be appropriate? And while you're at it, ask him if you might be missing any signs he is sending your way.

It's one thing to miss a message from your wife about cleaning up a room. It's something else entirely to miss one from God about the destiny of your life.

6

"I WILL LET YOU CHOOSE"

God's Promise Through the Two Crosses

There Jesus was nailed to the cross,
and on each side of him a man was also nailed to a cross.

JOHN 19:18 CEV

The prison has been stormed,
and the gates of the prison have been opened,
but unless we leave our prison cells and
go forward into the light of freedom,
we are still unredeemed in actuality.

DONALD BLOESCH

On the wood of the Cross the world was saved all at once,
and whoever is lost loses himself,
because he will not receive the Saviour,
because he falls again and repeats the fall of Adam.

COUNT NIKOLAUS LUDWIG VON ZINZENDORF

Meet Edwin Thomas, a master of the stage. During the latter half of the 1800s, this small man with the huge voice had few rivals. Debuting in *Richard III* at the age of fifteen, he quickly established himself as a premier Shakespearean actor. In New York he performed *Hamlet* for one hundred consecutive nights. In London he won the approval of the tough British critics. When it came to tragedy on the stage, Edwin Thomas was in a select group.

When it came to tragedy in life, the same could be said as well.

Edwin had two brothers, John and Junius. Both were actors, although neither rose to his stature. In 1863, the three siblings united their talents to perform *Julius Caesar.* The fact that Edwin's brother John took the role of Brutus was an eerie harbinger of what awaited the brothers—and the nation—two years hence.

For this John who played the assassin in *Julius Caesar* is the same John who took the role of assassin in Ford's Theatre. On a crisp April night in 1865, he stole quietly into the rear of a box in the Washington theater and fired a bullet at the head of Abraham

Lincoln. Yes, the last name of the brothers was Booth—Edwin Thomas Booth and John Wilkes Booth.

Edwin was never the same after that night. Shame from his brother's crime drove him into retirement. He might never have returned to the stage had it not been for a twist of fate at a New Jersey train station. Edwin was awaiting his coach when a well-dressed young man, pressed by the crowd, lost his footing and fell between the platform and a moving train. Without hesitation, Edwin locked a leg around a railing, grabbed the man, and pulled him to safety. After the sighs of relief, the young man recognized the famous Edwin Booth.

Edwin, however, didn't recognize the young man he'd rescued. That knowledge came weeks later in a letter, a letter he carried in his pocket to the grave. A letter from General Adams Budeau, chief secretary to General Ulysses S. Grant. A letter thanking Edwin Booth for saving the life of the child of an American hero, Abraham Lincoln. How ironic that while one brother killed the president, the other brother saved the president's son. The boy Edwin Booth yanked to safety? Robert Todd Lincoln.[1]

Edwin and James Booth. Same father, mother, profession, and passion—yet one chooses life, the other, death. How could it happen? I don't know, but it does. Though their story is dramatic, it's not unique.

Abel and Cain, both sons of Adam. Abel chooses God. Cain chooses murder. And God lets him.

Abraham and Lot, both pilgrims in Canaan. Abraham chooses God. Lot chooses Sodom. And God lets him.

David and Saul, both kings of Israel. David chooses God. Saul chooses power. And God lets him.

Peter and Judas, both deny their Lord. Peter seeks mercy. Judas seeks death. And God lets him.

In every age of history, on every page of Scripture, the truth is revealed: God allows us to make our own choices.

And no one delineates this more clearly than Jesus. According to him, we can choose:

a narrow gate or a wide gate (Matt. 7:13–14)

a narrow road or a wide road (Matt. 7:13–14)

the big crowd or the small crowd (Matt. 7:13–14)

We can choose to:

build on rock or sand (Matt. 7:24–27)

serve God or riches (Matt. 6:24)

be numbered among the sheep or the goats (Matt. 25:32–33)

"Then they [those who rejected God] will go away to eternal punishment, but the righteous to eternal life" (Matt. 25:46 NIV).

God gives eternal choices, and these choices have eternal consequences.

Isn't this the reminder of Calvary's trio? Ever wonder why there were two crosses next to Christ? Why not six or ten? Ever wonder why Jesus was in the center? Why not on the far right or far left? Could it be that the two crosses on the hill symbolize one of God's greatest gifts? The gift of choice.

The two criminals have so much in common. Convicted by the

same system. Condemned to the same death. Surrounded by the same crowd. Equally close to the same Jesus. In fact, they begin with the same sarcasm: "The two criminals also said cruel things to Jesus" (Matt. 27:44 CEV).

But one changed.

> One of the criminals on a cross began to shout insults at Jesus: "Aren't you the Christ? Then save yourself and us." But the other criminal stopped him and said, "You should fear God! You are getting the same punishment he is. We are punished justly, getting what we deserve for what we did. But this man has done nothing wrong." Then he said, "Jesus, remember me when you come into your kingdom." Jesus said to him, "I tell you the truth, today you will be with me in paradise." (Luke 23:39–43)

Much has been said about the prayer of the penitent thief, and it certainly warrants our admiration. But while we rejoice at the thief who changed, dare we forget the one who didn't? *What about him, Jesus? Wouldn't a personal invitation be appropriate? Wouldn't a word of persuasion be timely?*

Does not the shepherd leave the ninety-nine sheep and pursue the one lost? Does not the housewife sweep the house until the lost coin is found? Yes, the shepherd does, the housewife does, but the father of the prodigal, remember, does nothing.

The sheep was lost innocently.

The coin was lost irresponsibly.

But the prodigal son left intentionally.

The father gave him the choice. Jesus gave both criminals the same.

There are times when God sends thunder to stir us. There are times when God sends blessings to lure us. But then there are times when God sends nothing but silence as he honors us with the freedom to choose where we spend eternity.

And what an honor it is! In so many areas of life we have no choice. Think about it. You didn't choose your gender. You didn't choose your siblings. You didn't choose your race or place of birth.

Sometimes our lack of choices angers us. "It's not fair," we say. It's not fair that I was born in poverty or that I sing so poorly or that I run so slowly. But the scales of life were forever tipped on the side of fairness when God planted a tree in the Garden of Eden. All complaints were silenced when Adam and his descendants were given free will, the freedom to make whatever eternal choice we desire. Any injustice in this life is offset by the honor of choosing our destiny in the next.

Wouldn't you agree? Would you have wanted otherwise? Would you have preferred the opposite? You choose everything in this life, and he chooses where you spend the next? You choose the size of your nose, the color of your hair, and your DNA structure, and he chooses where you spend eternity? Is that what you would prefer?

It would have been nice if God had let us order life like we order a meal. I'll take good health and a high IQ. I'll pass on the music skills, but give me a fast metabolism . . . Would've been nice. But it didn't happen. When it came to your life on earth, you weren't given a voice or a vote.

But when it comes to life after death, you were. In my book that seems like a good deal. Wouldn't you agree?

Have we been given any greater privilege than that of choice?

Not only does this privilege offset any injustice, the gift of free will can offset any mistakes.

Think about the thief who repented. Though we know little about him, we know this: He made some bad mistakes in life. He chose the wrong crowd, the wrong morals, the wrong behavior. But would you consider his life a waste? Is he spending eternity reaping the fruit of all the bad choices he made? No, just the opposite. He is enjoying the fruit of the one good choice he made. In the end all his bad choices were redeemed by a solitary good one.

You've made some bad choices in life, haven't you? You've chosen the wrong friends, maybe the wrong career, even the wrong spouse. You look back over your life and say, "If only . . . if only I could make up for those bad choices." You can. One good choice for eternity offsets a thousand bad ones on earth.

The choice is yours.

How can two brothers be born of the same mother, grow up in the same home, and one choose life and the other choose death? I don't know, but they do.

How could two men see the same Jesus and one choose to mock him and the other choose to pray to him? I don't know, but they did.

And when one prayed, Jesus loved him enough to save him. And when the other mocked, Jesus loved him enough to let him.

He allowed him the choice.

He does the same for you.

7

"I WILL NOT ABANDON YOU"

God's Promise in the Path

Not only is this so,
but we also rejoice in God through our Lord Jesus Christ,
through whom we have now received reconciliation.

ROMANS 5:11 NIV

Sin in the biblical perspective is positive rebellion.

DONALD BLOESCH

For he has rescued us from the dominion of darkness
and brought us into the kingdom of the Son he loves.

COLOSSIANS 1:13 NIV

Man does, indeed, need a radical change of heart;
he needs to begin to hate his sin instead of loving it,
and to love God instead of hating him; he needs, in a word,
to be reconciled to God. And the place, above all others,
where this change takes place is at the foot of the cross,
when he apprehends something of the hatred of God for sin
and his indescribable love for the sinner.

J. N. D. ANDERSON

Five-year-old Madeline climbed into her father's lap.

"Did you have enough to eat?" he asked her.

She smiled and patted her tummy. "I can't eat any more."

"Did you have some of your Grandma's pie?"

"A whole piece!"

Joe looked across the table at his mom. "Looks like you filled us up. Don't think we'll be able to do anything tonight but go to bed."

Madeline put her little hands on either side of his big face. "Oh, but, Poppa, this is Christmas Eve. You said we could dance."

Joe feigned a poor memory. "Did I now? Why, I don't remember saying anything about dancing."

Grandma smiled and shook her head as she began clearing the table.

"But, Poppa," Madeline pleaded, "we always dance on Christmas Eve. Just you and me, remember?"

A smile burst from beneath his thick mustache. "Of course I remember, darling. How could I forget?"

And with that he stood and took her hand in his, and for a moment, just a moment, his wife was alive again, and the two were walking into the *den to spend another night before Christmas as they had spent so many, dancing away the evening.*

They would have danced the rest of their lives, but then came the surprise pregnancy and the complications. Madeline survived. But her mother did not. And Joe, the thick-handed butcher from Minnesota, was left to raise his Madeline alone.

"Come on, Poppa." She tugged on his hand. "Let's dance before everyone arrives." She was right. Soon the doorbell would ring and the relatives would fill the floor and the night would be past.

But, for now, it was just Poppa and Madeline.

✣

The love of a parent for a child is a mighty force. Consider the couple with their newborn child. The infant offers his parents absolutely nothing. No money. No skill. No words of wisdom. If he had pockets, they would be empty. To see an infant lying in a bassinet is to see utter helplessness. What is there to love?

Whatever it is, Mom and Dad find it. Just look at Mom's face as she nurses her baby. Just watch Dad's eyes as he cradles the child. And just try to harm or speak evil of the infant. If you do, you'll encounter a mighty strength, for the love of a parent is a mighty force.

Jesus once asked, if we humans who are sinful have such a love, how much more does God, the sinless and selfless Father, love us?[1] But what happens when the love isn't returned? What happens to the heart of the father when his child turns away?

✣

Rebellion flew into Joe's world like a Minnesota blizzard. About the time she was old enough to drive, Madeline decided she was old enough to lead her life. And that life did not include her father.

"I should have seen it coming," Joe would later say, "but for the life of me I didn't." He didn't know what to do. He didn't know how to handle the pierced nose and the tight shirts. He didn't understand the late nights and the poor grades. And, most of all, he didn't know when to speak and when to be quiet.

She, on the other hand, had it all figured out. She knew when to speak to her father—never. She knew when to be quiet—always. The pattern was reversed, however, with the lanky, tattooed kid from down the street. He was no good, and Joe knew it.

And there was no way he was going to allow his daughter to spend Christmas Eve with that kid.

"You'll be with us tonight, young lady. You'll be at your grandma's house eating your grandma's pie. You'll be with us on Christmas Eve."

Though they were at the same table, they might as well have been on different sides of town. Madeline played with her food and said nothing. Grandma tried to talk to Joe, but he was in no mood to chat. Part of him was angry; part of him was heartbroken. And the rest of him would have given anything to know how to talk to this girl who once sat on his lap.

Soon the relatives arrived, bringing with them a welcome end to the awkward silence. As the room filled with noise and people, Joe stayed on one side, Madeline sat sullenly on the other.

"Put on the music, Joe," reminded one of his brothers. And so he did. Thinking she would be honored, he turned and walked toward his daughter. "Will you dance with your poppa tonight?"

The way she huffed and turned, you'd have thought he'd insulted her.

In full view of the family, she walked out the front door and marched down the sidewalk. Leaving her father alone.

Very much alone.

✣

According to the Bible we have done the same. We have spurned the love of our Father. "Each of us has gone his own way" (Isa. 53:6).

Paul takes our rebellion a step further. We have done more than turn away, he says; we have turned *against*. "We were living against God" (Rom. 5:6).

He speaks even more bluntly in verse 10: "We were God's enemies." Harsh words, don't you think? An enemy is an adversary. One who offends, not out of ignorance, but by intent. Does this describe us? Have we ever been enemies of God? Have we ever turned against our Father?

Have you . . .

ever done something, knowing God wouldn't want you to do it?

ever hurt one of his children or part of creation?

ever supported or applauded the work of his adversary, the devil?

ever turned against your heavenly Father in public?

If so, have you not taken the role of an enemy?

So how does God react when we become his enemies?

✣

Madeline came back that night but not for long. Joe never faulted her for leaving. After all, what's it like being the daughter of a butcher? In their last days together he tried so hard. He made her favorite dinner—she didn't want to eat. He invited her to a movie—she stayed in her room. He bought her a new dress—she didn't even say thank you. And then there was that spring day he left work early to be at the house when she arrived home from school.

Wouldn't you know that was the day she never came home.

A friend saw her and her boyfriend in the vicinity of the bus station. The authorities confirmed the purchase of a ticket to Chicago; where she went from there was anybody's guess.

✣

The most notorious road in the world is the Via Dolorosa, "the Way of Sorrows." According to tradition, it is the route Jesus took from Pilate's hall to Calvary. The path is marked by stations frequently used by Christians for their devotions. One station marks the passing of Pilate's verdict. Another, the appearance of Simon to carry the cross. Two stations commemorate the stumble of Christ, another the words of Christ. There are fourteen stations in all, each one a reminder of the events of Christ's final journey.

Is the route accurate? Probably not. When Jerusalem was destroyed in A.D. 70 and again in A.D. 135, the streets of the city were destroyed. As a result, no one knows the exact route Christ followed that Friday.

But we do know where the path actually began.

The path began, not in the court of Pilate, but in the halls of heaven. The Father began his journey when he left his home in search of us. Armed with nothing more than a passion to win your heart, he came looking. His desire was singular—to bring his children home. The Bible has a word for this quest: *reconciliation.*

"God was in Christ reconciling the world to Himself" (2 Cor. 5:19 NKJV). The Greek word for *reconcile* means "to render something otherwise."[2] Reconciliation restiches the unraveled, reverses the rebellion, rekindles the cold passion.

Reconciliation touches the shoulder of the wayward and woos him homeward.

The path to the cross tells us exactly how far God will go to call us back.

The scrawny boy with the tattoos had a cousin. The cousin worked the night shift at a convenience store south of Houston. For a few bucks a month, he would let the runaways stay in his apartment at night, but they had to be out during the day.

Which was fine with them. They had big plans. He was going to be a mechanic, and Madeline just knew she could get a job at a department store. Of course he knew nothing about cars, and she knew even less about getting a job—but you don't think of things like that when you're intoxicated on freedom.

After a couple of weeks, the cousin changed his mind. And the day he announced his decision, the boyfriend announced his. Madeline found herself facing the night with no place to sleep or hand to hold.

It was the first of many such nights.

A woman in the park told her about the homeless shelter near the bridge. For a couple of bucks she could get a bowl of soup and a cot. A couple of bucks was about all she had. She used her backpack as a pillow and jacket as a blanket. The room was so rowdy it was hard to sleep. Madeline turned her face to the wall and, for the first time in several days, thought of the whiskered face of her father as he would kiss her good night. But as her eyes began to water, she refused to cry. She pushed the memory deep inside and determined not to think about home.

She'd gone too far to go back.

The next morning the girl in the cot beside her showed her a fistful of tips she'd made from dancing on tables. "This is the last night I'll have to stay here," she said. "Now I can pay for my own place. They told me they are looking for another girl. You should come by." She reached into her pocket and pulled out a matchbook. "Here's the address."

Madeline's stomach turned at the thought. All she could do was mumble, "I'll think about it."

She spent the rest of the week on the streets looking for work. At the end of the week when it was time to pay her bill at the shelter, she reached into her pocket and pulled out the matchbook. It was all she had left.

"I won't be staying tonight," she said and walked out the door.

Hunger has a way of softening convictions.

✣

Pride and shame. You'd never know they are sisters. They appear so different. Pride puffs out her chest. Shame hangs her head. Pride boasts. Shame hides. Pride seeks to be seen. Shame seeks to be avoided.

But don't be fooled, the emotions have the same parentage. And the emotions have the same impact. They keep you from your Father.

Pride says, "You're too good for him."

Shame says, "You're too bad for him."

Pride drives you away.

Shame keeps you away.

If pride is what goes before a fall, then shame is what keeps you from getting up after one.

✣

If Madeline knew anything, she knew how to dance. Her father had taught her. Now men the age of her father watched her. She didn't rationalize it—she just didn't think about it. Madeline simply did her work and took their dollars.

She might have never thought about it, except for the letters. The cousin brought them. Not one, or two, but a box full. All addressed to her. All from her father.

"Your old boyfriend must have squealed on you. These come two or three a week," complained the cousin. "Give him your address." Oh, but she couldn't do that. He might find her.

Nor could she bear to open the envelopes. She knew what they said; he wanted her home. But if he knew what she was doing, he would not be writing.

It seemed less painful not to read them. So she didn't. Not that week, nor the next when the cousin brought more, nor the next when he came again. She kept them in the dressing room at the club, organized according to postmark. She ran her finger over the top of each but couldn't bring herself to open one.

Most days Madeline was able to numb the emotions. Thoughts of home and thoughts of shame were shoved into the same part of her heart. But there were occasions when the thoughts were too strong to resist.

Like the time she saw a dress in the clothing store window. A dress the same color as one her father had purchased for her. A dress that had been far too plain for her. With much reluctance she had put it on and stood with him before the mirror. "My, you are as tall as I am," he had told her. She had stiffened at his touch.

Seeing her weary face reflected in the store window, Madeline realized she'd give a thousand dresses to feel his arm again. She left the store and resolved not to pass by it again.

In time the leaves fell and the air chilled. The mail came and the cousin complained and the stack of letters grew. Still she refused to send him an address. And she refused to read a letter.

Then a few days before Christmas Eve another letter arrived. Same shape. Same color. But this one had no postmark. And it was not delivered by the cousin. It was sitting on her dressing room table.

"A couple of days ago a big man stopped by and asked me to give this to you," explained one of the other dancers. "Said you'd understand the message."

"He was here?" she asked anxiously.

The woman shrugged, "Suppose he had to be."

Madeline swallowed hard and looked at the envelope. She opened it and removed the card. "I know where you are," it read. "I know what you do. This doesn't change the way I feel. What I've said in each letter is still true."

"But I don't know what you've said," Madeline declared. She pulled a letter from the top of the stack and read it. Then a second and a third. Each letter had the same sentence. Each sentence asked the same question.

In a matter of moments the floor was littered with paper and her face was streaked with tears.

Within an hour she was on a bus. "I just might make it in time."

She barely did.

The relatives were starting to leave. Joe was helping grandma in the kitchen when his brother called from the suddenly quiet den. "Joe, someone is here to see you."

Joe stepped out of the kitchen and stopped. In one hand the girl held a backpack. In the other she held a card. Joe saw the question in her eyes.

"The answer is 'yes,'" she said to her father. "If the invitation is still good, the answer is 'yes.'"

Joe swallowed hard. "Oh my. The invitation is good."

And so the two danced again on Christmas Eve.

On the floor, near the door, rested a letter with Madeline's name and her father's request.

"Will you come home and dance with your poppa again?"

8

"I WILL GIVE YOU MY ROBE"

God's Promise in the Garment

But Christ without guilt . . . took upon himself our punishment,
in order that he might thus expiate our guilt,
and do away with our punishment.

Augustine

For Christ died for sins once for all,
the righteous for the unrighteous,
to bring you to God.

1 Peter 3:18 niv

This is the mystery of the riches of divine grace for sinners;
for by a wonderful exchange our sins are now not ours but Christ's,
and Christ's righteousness is not Christ's but ours.

Martin Luther

The maître d' wouldn't change his mind. He didn't care that this was our honeymoon. It didn't matter that the evening at the classy country club restaurant was a wedding gift. He couldn't have cared less that Denalyn and I had gone without lunch to save room for dinner. All of this was immaterial in comparison to the looming problem.

I wasn't wearing a jacket.

Didn't know I needed one. I thought a sport shirt was sufficient. It was clean and tucked in. But Mr. Black-Tie with the French accent was unimpressed. He seated everyone else. Mr. and Mrs. Debonair were given a table. Mr. and Mrs. Classier-Than-You were seated. But Mr. and Mrs. Didn't-Wear-a-Jacket?

If I'd had another option, I wouldn't have begged. But I didn't. The hour was late. Other restaurants were closed or booked, and we were hungry. "There's got to be something you can do," I pleaded. He looked and me, then at Denalyn, and let out a long sigh that puffed his cheeks.

"All right, let me see."

He disappeared into the cloakroom and emerged with a jacket. "Put this on." I did. The sleeves were too short. The shoulders were too tight. And the color was lime green. But I didn't complain. I had a jacket, and we were taken to a table. (Don't tell anyone, but I took it off when the food came.)

For all the inconvenience of the evening, we ended up with a great dinner and an even greater parable.

I needed a jacket, but all I had was a prayer. The fellow was too kind to turn me away but too loyal to lower the standard. So the very one who required a jacket gave me a jacket, and we were given a table.

Isn't this what happened at the cross? Seats at God's table are not available to the sloppy. But who among us is anything but? Unkempt morality. Untidy with truth. Careless with people. Our moral clothing is in disarray. Yes, the standard for sitting at God's table is high, but the love of God for his children is higher. So he offers a gift.

Not a lime-colored jacket but a robe. A seamless robe. Not a garment pulled out of a cloakroom but a robe worn by his Son, Jesus.

Scripture says little about the clothes Jesus wore. We know what his cousin John the Baptist wore. We know what the religious leaders wore. But the clothing of Christ is nondescript: neither so humble as to touch hearts nor so glamorous as to turn heads.

One reference to Jesus' garments is noteworthy. "They divided his clothes among the four of them. They also took his robe, but it was seamless, woven in one piece from the top. So they said, 'Let's not tear it but throw dice to see who gets it'" (John 19:23–24 NLT).

It must have been Jesus' finest possession. Jewish tradition called for a mother to make such a robe and present it to her son as a departure gift when he left home. Had Mary done this for Jesus? We don't know. But we do know the tunic was without seam, woven from top to bottom. Why is this significant?

Scripture often describes our behavior as the clothes we wear. Peter urges us to be "clothed with humility" (1 Pet. 5:5 NKJV). David speaks of evil people who clothe themselves "with cursing" (Ps. 109:18 NKJV). Garments can symbolize character, and like his garment, Jesus' character was seamless. Coordinated. Unified. He was like his robe: uninterrupted perfection.

"Woven . . . from the top." Jesus wasn't led by his own mind; he was led by the mind of his Father. Listen to his words:

"The Son can do nothing on his own, but only what he sees the Father doing; for whatever the Father does, the Son does likewise" (John 5:19 NRSV).

"I can do nothing on my own. As I hear, I judge" (John 5:30 NRSV).

The character of Jesus was a seamless fabric woven from heaven to earth . . . from God's thoughts to Jesus' actions. From God's tears to Jesus' compassion. From God's word to Jesus' response. All one piece. All a picture of the character of Jesus.

But when Christ was nailed to the cross, he took off his robe of seamless perfection and assumed a different wardrobe, the wardrobe of indignity.

The indignity of nakedness. Stripped before his own mother and loved ones. Shamed before his family.

The indignity of failure. For a few pain-filled hours, the religious leaders were the victors, and Christ appeared the loser. Shamed before his accusers.

Worst of all, he wore the *indignity of sin*. "He himself bore our sins in his body on the tree, so that we might die to sins and live for righteousness" (1 Pet. 2:24 NIV).

The clothing of Christ on the cross? Sin—yours and mine. The sins of all humanity.

I can remember my father explaining to me the reason a group of men on the side of the road wore striped clothing. "They're prisoners," he said. "They have broken the law and are serving time."

You want to know what stuck with me about these men? They never looked up. They never made eye contact. Were they ashamed? Probably so.

What they felt on the side of the road was what our Savior felt on the cross—disgrace. Every aspect of the crucifixion was intended not only to hurt the victim but to shame him. Death on a cross was usually reserved for the most vile offenders: slaves, murderers, assassins, and the like. The condemned person was marched through the city streets, shouldering his crossbar and wearing a placard about his neck that named his crime. At the execution site he was stripped and mocked.

Crucifixion was so abhorrent that Cicero wrote, "Let the very name of the cross be far away, not only from the body of a Roman citizen, but even from his thoughts, his eyes, his ears."[1]

Jesus was not only shamed before people, he was shamed before heaven.

Since he bore the sin of the murderer and adulterer, he felt the shame of the murderer and adulterer. Though he never lied, he bore the disgrace of a liar. Though he never cheated, he felt the embarrassment of a cheater. Since he bore the sin of the world, he felt the collective shame of the world.

It's no wonder that the Hebrew writer spoke of the "disgrace he bore" (Heb. 13:13 NLT).

While on the cross, Jesus felt the indignity and disgrace of a criminal. No, he was not guilty. No, he had not committed a sin. And, no, he did not deserve to be sentenced. But you and I were, we had, and we did. We were left in the same position I was with the maître d'—having nothing to offer but a prayer. Jesus, however, goes further than the maître d'. Can you imagine the restaurant host removing his tuxedo coat and offering it to me?

Jesus does. We're not talking about an ill-fitting, leftover jacket. He offers a robe of seamless purity and dons my patchwork coat of pride, greed, and selfishness. "He changed places with us" (Gal. 3:13). He wore our sin so we could wear his righteousness.

Though we come to the cross dressed in sin, we leave the cross dressed in the "coat of his strong love" (Isa. 59:17) and girded with a belt of "goodness and fairness" (Isa. 11:5) and clothed in "garments of salvation" (Isa. 61:10 NIV).

Indeed, we leave dressed in Christ himself. "You have all put on Christ as a garment" (Gal. 3:27 NEB).

It wasn't enough for him to prepare you a feast.

It wasn't enough for him to reserve you a seat.

It wasn't enough for him to cover the cost and provide the transportation to the banquet.

He did something more. He let you wear his own clothes so that you would be properly dressed.

He did that . . . just for you.

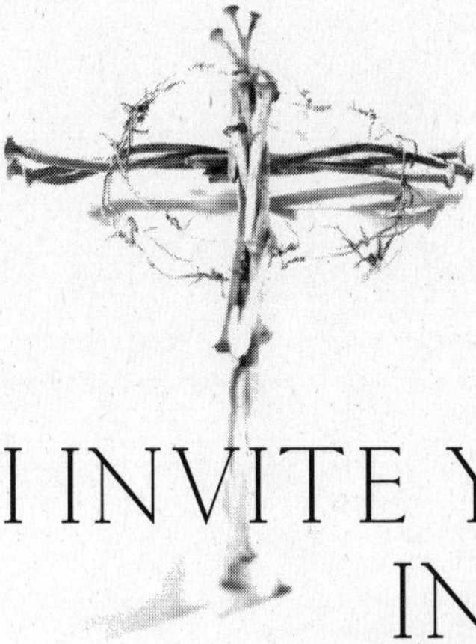

9

"I INVITE YOU INTO MY PRESENCE"

God's Promise Through the Torn Flesh

We can enter through a new and living way that
Jesus opened for us. It leads through the curtain—Christ's body.

HEBREWS 10:20

For through him we both have access
to the Father by one Spirit.

EPHESIANS 2:18 NIV

Let us then approach the throne of grace with confidence,
so that we may receive mercy and find grace
to help us in our time of need.

HEBREWS 4:16 NIV

Imagine a person standing in front of the White House. Better still, imagine yourself standing in front of the White House.

That's you on the sidewalk, peering through the fence, over the lawn, at the residence of the president. That's you—in fine form—hair in place and shoes shined. That's you turning toward the entrance. Your pace is brisk and stride sure. It should be. You have come to meet with the president.

You have a few matters you wish to discuss with him.

First, there is the matter of the fire hydrant in front of your house. Could they soften the red just a shade? It's too bright.

Then there's the issue of world peace. You are for it—would he create it?

And lastly, college tuition is too high. Could he call the admissions office of your daughter's school and ask them to lighten up? He might have some influence.

All worthy issues, correct? Won't take more than a few minutes. Besides, you brought him some cookies that he can share with the first lady and the first puppy. So with bag in hand and a smile on your face, you step up to the gate and announce to the guard, "I'd like to see the president please."

He asks for your name, and you give it. He looks at you and then at his list and says, "We have no record of your appointment."

"You have to have an appointment?"

"Yes."

"How do I get one?"

"Through his office staff."

"Could I have their number?"

"No, it's restricted."

"Then how can I get in?"

"It's better to wait until they call you."

"But they don't know me!"

The guard shrugs. "Then they probably won't call."

And so you sigh and turn and begin your journey home. Your questions are unanswered and your needs unmet.

And you were so close! Had the president stepped out onto the lawn, you could've waved, and he would've waved back. You were only yards from his front door . . . but you might as well have been miles. The two of you were separated by the fence and the guard.

Then there is the problem of the Secret Service. Had you somehow entered, they would have stopped you. The staff would have done the same. There were too many barriers.

And what about the invisible barriers? Barriers of time. (The president's too busy.) Barriers of status. (You have no clout.) Barriers of protocol. (You have to go through the right channels.) You leave the White House with nothing more than a hard lesson learned. You do not have access to the president. Your chat with the commander in chief? It ain't gonna happen. You'll have to take your problem about peace and your question about the fire hydrant with you.

That is, unless he takes the initiative. Unless he, spotting you on the sidewalk, takes pity on your plight and says to his chief of staff, "See that person with the sack of cookies? Go tell him I'd like to talk with him for a minute."

If he gives such a command, all the barriers will drop. The Oval Office will call the head of security. The head of security will call the guard, and the guard will call your name. "Guess what? I can't explain it, but the door to the Oval Office is wide open."

You stop and turn and straighten your shoulders and enter the same door where, only moments before, you were denied access. The guard is the same. The gates are the same. The security personnel are the same. But the situation is not the same. You can now go where before you could not.

And, what's more, *you* are not the same. You feel special, chosen. Why? Because the man up there saw you down here and made it possible for you to come in.

Yeah, you're right. It's a fanciful story. You and I both know when it comes to the president, don't hold your breath—no invitation will arrive. But when it comes to God, pick up your cookies and walk in, because it already has.

He has spotted you. He has heard you, and he has invited you. What once separated you has been removed: "Now in Christ Jesus, you who were far away from God are brought near" (Eph. 2:13). Nothing remains between you and God but an open door.

But how could this be? If we can't get in to see the president, how could we be granted an audience with God? What happened?

In a word, someone opened the curtain. Someone tore down the veil. Something happened in the death of Christ that opened the door for you and me. And that something is described by the writer of Hebrews.

> So, brothers and sisters, we are completely free to enter the Most Holy Place without fear because of the blood of Jesus' death. We can enter through a new and living way that Jesus opened for us. It leads through the curtain—Christ's body. (Heb. 10:19–20)

To the original readers, those last four words were explosive: "the curtain—Christ's body." According to the writer, the curtain equals Jesus. Hence, whatever happened to the flesh of Jesus happened to the curtain. What happened to his flesh? It was torn. Torn by the whips, torn by the thorns. Torn by the weight of the cross and the point of the nails. But in the horror of his torn flesh, we find the splendor of the open door.

"But Jesus cried out again in a loud voice and died. Then the curtain in the Temple was torn into two pieces, from the top to the bottom" (Matt. 27:50–51).

The curtain is nothing short of the curtain of the Temple. The veil that hung before the Holy of Holies.

The Holy of Holies, you'll remember, was a part of the Temple no one could enter. Jewish worshipers could enter the outer court, but only the priests could enter the Holy Place. And no one, except the high priest on one day a year, entered the Holy of Holies. No one. Why? Because the shekinah glory—the glory of God—was present there.

If you were told you were free to enter the Oval Office of the White House, you would likely shake your head and chuckle, "You're one brick short of a load, buddy." Multiply your disbelief by a thousand, and you'll have an idea how a Jew would feel if someone told him he could enter the Holy of Holies. "Yeah, right. You're one bagel short of a dozen."

No one but the high priest entered the Holy of Holies. *No one*. To do so meant death. Two of Aaron's sons died when they entered the Holy of Holies in order to offer sacrifices to the Lord (Lev. 16:1–2). In no uncertain terms, the curtain declared: "This far and no farther!"

What did fifteen hundred years of a curtain-draped Holy of Holies communicate? Simple. God is holy . . . separate from us and unapproachable. Even Moses was told, "You cannot see my face, because no one can see me and live" (Exod. 33:20). God is holy, and we are sinners, and there is a distance between us.

Isn't this our problem? We know God is good. We know we are not, and we feel far from God. The ancient words of Job are ours, "If only there were a mediator who could bring us together" (Job 9:33 NLT).

Oh, but there is! Jesus hasn't left us with an unapproachable God. Yes, God is holy. Yes, we are sinful. But, yes, yes, yes, Jesus is our mediator. "There is one God and one mediator between God and men, the man Christ Jesus" (1 Tim. 2:5 NIV). Is not a mediator one who "goes between"? Wasn't Jesus the curtain between us and God? And wasn't his flesh torn?

What appeared to be the cruelty of man was actually the sovereignty of God. Matthew tells us: "And when Jesus had cried out again in a loud voice, he gave up his spirit. *At that moment* the curtain of the temple was torn in two from top to bottom" (27:50–51 NIV, italics mine).

It's as if the hands of heaven had been gripping the veil, waiting for this moment. Keep in mind the size of the curtain—sixty feet tall and thirty feet wide.[1] One instant it was whole; the next it was ripped in two from top to bottom. No delay. No hesitation.

What did the torn curtain mean? For the Jews it meant no more barrier between them and the Holy of Holies. No more priests to go between them and God. No more animal sacrifices to atone for their sins.

And for us? What did the torn curtain signify for us?

We are welcome to enter into God's presence—any day, any time. God has removed the barrier that separates us from him. The barrier of sin? Down. He has removed the curtain.

But we have a tendency to put the barrier back up. Though there is no curtain in a temple, there is a curtain in the heart. Like the ticks on the clock are the mistakes of the heart. And sometimes, no, oftentimes, we allow those mistakes to keep us from God. Our guilty conscience becomes a curtain that separates us from God.

As a result we hide from our Master.

That's exactly what my dog, Salty, does. He knows he isn't supposed to get into the trash. But let the house be human free, and the dark side of Salty takes over. If there is food in a trash can, the temptation is too great. He will find it and feast.

That's what he had done the other day. When I came home, he was nowhere to be found. I saw the toppled trash, but I didn't see Salty. At first I got mad, but I got over it. If I was cooped up all day with only dog food to eat, I might rummage a bit myself. I cleaned up the mess and went about the day and forgot about it.

Salty didn't. He kept his distance. When I finally saw him, his tail was between his legs, and his ears were drooping. Then I realized, "He thinks I'm mad at him. He doesn't know I've already dealt with his mistake."

May I state the obvious application? God isn't angry with you. He has already dealt with your mistake.

Somewhere, sometime, somehow you got tangled up in garbage, and you've been avoiding God. You've allowed a veil of guilt to come between you and your Father. You wonder if you could ever feel close to God again. The message of the torn flesh is *you can.* God welcomes you. God is not avoiding you. God is not resisting you. The curtain is down, the door is open, and God invites you in.

Don't trust your conscience. Trust the cross. The blood has been spilt and the veil has been split. You are welcome in God's presence. And you don't even have to bring cookies.

10

"I UNDERSTAND YOUR PAIN"

God's Promise in the Wine-Soaked Sponge

Praise be to the God and Father of our Lord Jesus Christ,
the Father of compassion and the God of all comfort,
who comforts us in all our troubles,
so that we can comfort those
in any trouble with the comfort we ourselves
have received from God. For just as the sufferings of Christ
flow over into our lives, so also through Christ our comfort overflows.

2 CORINTHIANS 1:3–5 NIV

For the LORD comforts his people
and will have compassion on his afflicted ones.

ISAIAH 49:13 NIV

For we do not have a high priest who is
unable to sympathize with our weaknesses,
but we have one who has been tempted in every way,
just as we are—yet was without sin.

HEBREWS 4:15 NIV

Jesus wept.

JOHN 11:35 NIV

Ever tried to convince a mouse not to worry? Ever succeeded in pacifying the panic of a rodent? If so, you are wiser than I. My attempt was not successful. My comforting words fell on tiny, deaf ears.

Not that the fellow deserved any kindness, mind you. Because of him, Denalyn screamed. Because of the scream, the garage shook. Because the garage shook, I was yanked out of dreamland and off my La-Z-Boy and called to defend my wife and country. I was proud to go. With shoulders high, I marched into the garage.

The mouse never had a chance. I know jujitsu, karate, tae kwan do and several other . . . uh, phrases. I've even watched self-defense infomercials. This mouse had met his match.

Besides, he was trapped in an empty trash can. How he got there only he knows, and he ain't telling. I know, I asked him. His only reply was a mad rush around the base of the can.

The poor guy was scared to the tip of his whiskers. And who wouldn't be? Imagine being caged in a plastic container and looking up only to see the large (albeit handsome) face of a human. Would be enough to make you chuck up your cheese.

"What are you going to do with him?" Denalyn asked, clutching my arm for courage.

"Don't worry, little darlin'," I replied with a swagger that made her swoon and would have made John Wayne jealous. "I'll go easy on the little fellow."

So off we went—the mouse, the trash can, and me, marching down the cul-de-sac toward an empty lot. "Stick with me, little guy. I'll have you home in no time." He didn't listen. You'd have thought we were walking to death row. Had I not placed a lid on the can, the furry fellow would have jumped out. "I'm not going to hurt you," I explained. "I'm going to release you. You got yourself into a mess; I'm going to get you out."

He never calmed down. He never sat still. He never—well, he never trusted me. Even at the last moment, when I tilted the can on the ground and set him free, did he turn around and say thank you? Did he invite me to his mouse house for a meal? No. He just ran. (Was it my imagination, or did I hear him shouting, "Get back! Get back! Max, the mouse-hater, is here"?)

Honestly. What would I have to do to win his trust? Learn to speak Mouse-agese? Grow beady eyes and a long tail? Get down in the trash with him? Thanks, but no thanks. I mean, the mouse was cute and all, but he wasn't worth that much.

Apparently you and I are.

You think it's absurd for a man to become a mouse? The journey from your house to a trash can is far shorter than the one from heaven to earth. But Jesus took it. Why?

He wants us to trust him.

Explore this thought with me for just a moment. Why did Jesus live on the earth as long as he did? Couldn't his life have been much shorter? Why not step into our world just long enough to die for our sins and then leave? Why not a sinless year or week? Why did he have to live a life? To take on our sins is one thing, but to take on our sunburns, our sore throats? To experience death, yes—but to put up with life? To put up with long roads, long days, and short tempers? Why did he do it?

Because he wants you to trust him.

Even his final act on earth was intended to win your trust.

> Later, knowing that all was now completed, and so that the Scripture would be fulfilled, Jesus said, "I am thirsty." A jar of wine vinegar was there, so they soaked a sponge in it, put the sponge on a stalk of the hyssop plant, and lifted it to Jesus' lips. When he had received the drink, Jesus said, "It is finished." With that, he bowed his head and gave up his spirit. (John 19:28–30 NIV)

This is the final act of Jesus' life. In the concluding measure of his earthly composition, we hear the sounds of a thirsty man.

And through his thirst—through a sponge and a jar of cheap wine—he leaves a final appeal.

"You can trust me."

Jesus. Lips cracked and mouth of cotton. Throat so dry he couldn't swallow, and voice so hoarse he could scarcely speak. He is thirsty. To find the last time moisture touched these lips you need to rewind a dozen hours to the meal in the upper room. Since tasting that cup of wine, Jesus has been beaten, spat upon, bruised, and cut. He has been a cross-carrier and sin-bearer, and no liquid has salved his throat. He is thirsty.

Why doesn't he do something about it? Couldn't he? Did he not cause jugs of water to be jugs of wine? Did he not make a wall out of the Jordan River and two walls out of the Red Sea? Didn't he, with one word, banish the rain and calm the waves? Doesn't Scripture say that he "turned the desert into pools" (Ps. 107:35 NIV) and "the hard rock into springs" (Ps. 114:8 NIV)?

Did God not say, "I will pour water on him who is thirsty" (Isa. 44:3 NKJV)?

If so, why does Jesus endure thirst?

While we are asking this question, add a few more. Why did he grow weary in Samaria (John 4:6), disturbed in Nazareth (Mark 6:6), and angry in the Temple (John 2:15)? Why was he sleepy in the boat on the Sea of Galilee (Mark 4:38), sad at the tomb of Lazarus (John 11:35), and hungry in the wilderness (Matt. 4:2)?

Why? And why did he grow thirsty on the cross?

He didn't have to suffer thirst. At least, not to the level he did. Six hours earlier he'd been offered drink, but he refused it.

> They brought Jesus to the place called Golgotha (which means The Place of the Skull). Then they offered him wine mixed with myrrh, but *he did not take it*. And they crucified him. Dividing up his clothes, they cast lots to see what each would get. (Mark 15:22–24 NIV, italics mine)

Before the nail was pounded, a drink was offered. Mark says the wine was mixed with myrrh. Matthew described it as wine mixed with gall. Both myrrh and gall contain sedative properties that numb the senses. But Jesus refused them. He refused to be stupefied by the drugs, opting instead to feel the full force of his suffering.

Why? Why did he endure all these feelings? *Because he knew you would feel them too.*

He knew you would be weary, disturbed, and angry. He knew you'd be sleepy, grief-stricken, and hungry. He knew you'd face pain. If not the pain of the body, the pain of the soul . . . pain too sharp for any drug. He knew you'd face thirst. If not a thirst for water, at least a thirst for truth, and the truth we glean from the image of a thirsty Christ is—he understands.

And because he understands, we can come to him.

Wouldn't his lack of understanding keep us from him? Doesn't the lack of understanding keep us from others? Suppose you were discouraged at your financial state. You need some guidance from a sympathetic friend. Would you go to the son of a zillionaire? (Remember, you're asking for guidance, not a handout.) Would you approach someone who inherited a fortune? Probably not. Why? He would not understand. He's likely never been where you are, so he can't relate to how you feel.

Jesus, however, has and can. He has been where you are and can relate to how you feel. And if his life on earth doesn't convince you, his death on the cross should. He understands what you are going through. Our Lord does not patronize us or scoff at our needs. He responds "generously to all without finding fault"

(James 1:5 NIV). How can he do this? No one penned it more clearly than did the author of Hebrews.

> Jesus understands every weakness of ours, because he was tempted in every way that we are. But he did not sin! So whenever we are in need, we should come bravely before the throne of our merciful God. There we will be treated with undeserved kindness, and we will find help. (Heb. 4:15–16 CEV)

Why did the throat of heaven grow raw? So we would know that he understands; so all who struggle would hear his invitation: "You can trust me."

The word *trust* does not appear in the passage about the wine and sponge, but we do find a phrase that makes it easier to trust. Look at the sentence prior to the declaration of thirst: "So that the Scripture would be fulfilled, Jesus said, 'I am thirsty'" (John 19:28 NIV). In that verse John gives us the motive behind Jesus' words. Our Lord was concerned with the fulfillment of Scripture. In fact, the fulfillment of Scripture is a recurring theme in the passion. Consider this list:

> The betrayal of Jesus by Judas occurred "to bring about what the Scripture said." (John 13:18; see John 17:12)
>
> The gamble for the clothing took place "so that this Scripture would come true: 'They divided my clothes among them, and they threw lots for my clothing.'" (John 19:24)
>
> The legs of Christ were not broken "to make the Scripture come true: 'Not one of his bones will be broken.'" (John 19:36)

> The side of Jesus was pierced to fulfill the passage that says, "They will look at the one they stabbed." (John 19:37)

> John says the disciples were stunned by the empty tomb since "they did not yet understand from the Scriptures that Jesus must rise from the dead." (John 20:9)

Why the recurring references to Scripture? Why, in his final moments, was Jesus determined to fulfill prophecy? He knew we would doubt. He knew we would question. And since he did not want our heads to keep his love from our hearts, he used his final moments to offer proof that he was the Messiah. He systematically fulfilled centuries-old prophecies.

Every important detail of the great tragedy had been written down beforehand:

- the betrayal by a familiar friend (Ps. 41:9)
- the forsaking of the disciples through being offended at him (Ps. 31:11)
- the false accusation (Ps. 35:11)
- the silence before his judges (Isa. 53:7)
- being proven guiltless (Isa. 53:9)
- being included with sinners (Isa. 53:12)
- being crucified (Ps. 22:16)
- the mockery of the spectators (Ps. 109:25)
- the taunt of nondeliverance (Ps. 22:7–8)
- the gambling for his garments (Ps. 22:18)

- the prayer for his enemies (Isa. 53:12)
- being forsaken by God (Ps. 22:1)
- the yielding of his spirit into the hands of his Father (Ps. 31:5)
- the bones not broken (Ps. 34:20)
- the burial in a rich man's tomb (Isa. 53:9)

Did you know that in his life Christ fulfilled 332 distinct prophecies in the Old Testament? What are the mathematical possibilities of all these prophecies being fulfilled in the life of one man?

$$\frac{1}{\begin{array}{c}840,000,000,000,000,000,000,000,\\ 000,000,000,000,000,000,000,000,000,\\ 000,000,000,000,000,000,000,000,000,000,\\ 000,000,000,000,000,000\end{array}}$$

(That's ninety-seven zeroes!)[1] Amazing!

Why did Jesus proclaim his thirst from the cross? To lay just one more plank on a sturdy bridge over which a doubter could walk.[2] His confession of thirst is a signal for all who seek it—he is the Messiah.

His final act, then, is a warm word for the cautious: "You can trust in me."

Don't we need someone to trust? And don't we need someone to trust who is bigger than we are? Aren't we tired of trusting the people of this earth for understanding? Aren't we weary of trusting the things of this earth for strength? A drowning sailor doesn't call on another drowning sailor for help. A prisoner doesn't beg another prisoner to set him free. A pauper knows better than to beg from another pauper. He knows he needs someone who is stronger than he is.

Jesus' message through the wine-soaked sponge is this: I am that person. Trust me.

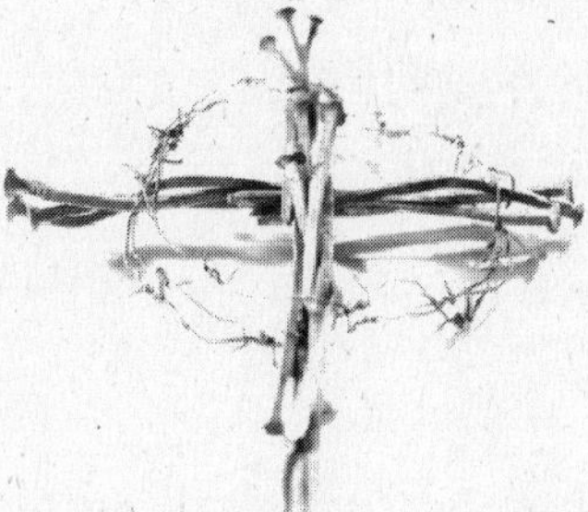

11

"I HAVE REDEEMED YOU AND I WILL KEEP YOU"

God's Promise in the Blood and Water

Christ "offered for all time a single sacrifice for sins"
and "by a single offering he has perfected
for all time those who are sanctified."

HEBREWS 10:12, 14 NRSV

This is love: not that we loved God,
but that he loved us and sent his Son
as an atoning sacrifice for our sins.

1 JOHN 4:10 NIV

Our position is such that we can be rescued from
eternal death and translated into
life only by total and unceasing substitution,
the substitution which God Himself undertakes on our behalf.

KARL BARTH

Yet though the work of Christ is finished for *the sinner,*
it is not yet finished in *the sinner.*

DONALD G. BLOESCH

My name was in the sports section of the newspaper this week. You had to search to find it, but it was there. Four pages into Tuesday's edition, midway down the sheet at the end of an article about the Texas Open Golf Tournament, there was my name. All nine letters' worth.

It was a first for me. My name has appeared in other parts of the paper for a variety of reasons, some of which I'm proud and some of which I'm not. But this was my first time in the sports section. It took over forty years, but I finally made it.

It was also my first sports award. I almost got one in middle school when I finished seventh in the discus throw. But they gave ribbons only up to sixth place, so I missed out. Got a few other awards along the way, but none for sports. Until yesterday. My first sports award.

Here is what happened. My friend Buddy is the director of golf at the course that hosts the PGA Texas Open. He asked if I'd like to play in the annual Pro-Am Tournament. I thought about it for three seconds and accepted.

The Pro-Am has a simple format. Each team has one pro and four amateurs. The low score from each of the amateurs is recorded. In other words, even on the holes where I stunk, if one of my partners did well, I did well. And that is exactly what happened on, oh let me count, seventeen out of eighteen holes.

Imagine the joy of such a game. Let's take a typical hole where I score an eight but Buddy or one of the other fellows scores a three. Guess which score is recorded? The three! Max's eight is forgotten and Buddy's birdie is remembered. A person could get used to this! I get credit for the good work of someone else simply by virtue of being on his team.

Hasn't Christ done the same for you?

What my team did for me on Monday, your Lord does for you every day of the week. Because of his performance, you close your daily round with a perfect score. Doesn't matter if you sprayed a few into the woods or shanked one into the water. What matters is that you showed up to play and joined the right foursome. In this case your foursome is pretty strong; it's you, the Father, the Son, and the Holy Spirit. A better team doesn't exist.

The two-dollar theological term for this is *positional sanctification.* Simply defined: You are given a prize, not because of what you do, but because of whom you know.

A second word was illustrated in that golf game. (What kind of mind is this—finding theology on a fairway?) Not only do you see a picture of positional sanctification; there is an equally clear portrait of *progressive sanctification.*

Remember my contribution? One out of eighteen holes. On one hole I made a par. My par went on the card and carried the team. Want to guess on which hole I made the par? The last one.

Though I offered so little, I improved with each hole. Buddy kept giving me tips and changing my grip until finally I made a contribution. I improved progressively.

The prize came because of Buddy's score. The improvement came because of Buddy's help.

Positional sanctification comes because of Christ's work *for* us.

Progressive sanctification comes because of Christ's work *in* us.

Both are gifts from God.

"With one sacrifice he made perfect forever those who are being made holy" (Heb. 10:14). See the blending of tenses? "He made perfect" (positional sanctification) those who are "being made holy" (progressive sanctification).

Positional and progressive sanctification. God's work for us and God's work in us. Neglect the first, and you grow fearful. Neglect the second, and you grow lazy. Both are essential, and both are seen in the moistened dirt at the base of the cross of Christ. Let's examine each of these more carefully.

God's work for us.

Listen to this passage. "But one of the soldiers stuck his spear into Jesus' side, and at once blood and water came out" (John 19:34). Even a casual student of Scripture notes the connection between blood and mercy. As far back as the son of Adam, worshipers knew "without the shedding of blood there is no forgiveness" (Heb. 9:22 NIV).

How Abel knew this truth is anyone's guess, but somehow he knew to offer more than prayers and crops. He knew to offer a life. He knew to pour out more than his heart and his desires; he knew to pour out blood. With a field as his temple and the ground as his altar, Abel became the first to do what millions would imitate. He offered a blood sacrifice for sins.

Those who followed suit form a long line: Abraham, Moses, Gideon, Samson, Saul, David . . . They knew the shedding of blood was necessary for the forgiveness of sins. Jacob knew it too; hence, the stones were stacked for the altar. Solomon knew it, and the Temple was built. Aaron knew it; therefore, the priesthood began. Haggai and Zechariah knew it; as a result, the Temple was built again.

But the line ended at the cross. What Abel sought to accomplish in the field, God achieved with his Son. What Abel began, Christ completed. After his sacrifice there would be no more sacrificial system because "he came as High Priest of this better system which we now have" (Heb. 9:11 TLB).

After Christ's sacrifice there would be no more need to shed blood. He "once for all took blood into that inner room, the Holy of Holies, and sprinkled it on the mercy seat; but it was not the blood of goats and calves. No, he took his own blood, and with it he, by himself, made sure of our eternal salvation" (Heb. 9:12 TLB).

The Son of God became the Lamb of God, the cross became the altar, and we were "made holy through the sacrifice Christ made in his body once and for all time" (Heb. 10:10).

What needed to be paid was paid. What had to be done was done. Innocent blood was required. Innocent blood was offered, once and for all time. Bury those five words deep in your heart. *Once and for all time.*

At the risk of sounding like an elementary school teacher, let me ask an elementary question. If the sacrifice has been offered once and for all time, need it be offered again?

Of course not. You are positionally sanctified. Just as the achievements of my team were credited to me, so the achievement of Jesus' blood is credited to us.

And just as my skills improved through the influence of a teacher, your life can improve the longer and closer you walk with Jesus. The work for us is complete, but the progressive work in us is ongoing.

If his work for us is seen in the blood, what might the water represent? You got it.

His work in us.

Remember the words of Jesus to the Samaritan woman? "The water I give will become a spring of water gushing up inside that person, giving eternal life" (John 4:14). Jesus offers, not a singular drink of water, but a perpetual artesian well! And the well isn't a hole in your backyard but the Holy Spirit of God in your heart.

> "If anyone believes in me, rivers of living water will flow out from that person's heart, as the Scripture says." Jesus was talking about the Holy Spirit. The Spirit had not yet been given, because Jesus had not yet been raised to glory. But later, those who believed in Jesus would receive the Spirit. (John 7:38–39)

Water, in this verse, is a picture of the Spirit of Jesus working *in* us. He's not working to save us, mind you; that work is done. He's working to change us. Here is how Paul phrased the process.

> Do the good things that *result from being saved,* obeying God with deep reverence, *shrinking back from all that might displease him. For God is at work within you,* helping you want to obey him, and then helping you do what he wants. (Phil. 2:12–13 TLB, italics mine)

As a result of "being saved" (the work of the blood), what do we do? We obey God "with deep reverence" and shrink back "from all that might displease him." Practically put, we love our neighbor and refrain from gossip. We refuse to cheat on taxes and spouses and do our best to love people who are tough to love. Do we do this in order to be saved? No. These are "the good things that result from being saved."

A similar dynamic occurs in marriage. Are a bride and groom ever more married than they are the first day? The vows are made and the certificate signed—could they be any more married than that?

Perhaps they could. Imagine them fifty years later. Four kids later. A trio of transfers and a cluster of valleys and victories later. After half a century of marriage, they finish each other's sentences and order each other's food. They even start looking alike after a while (a thought which troubles Denalyn deeply). Wouldn't they have to be more married on their fiftieth anniversary than on their wedding day?

Yet, on the other hand, how could they be? The marriage certificate hasn't matured. Ah, but the relationship has, and there is the difference. Technically, they are no more united than they were when they left the altar. But relationally, they are completely different.

Marriage is both a done deal and a daily development, something you did and something you do.

The same is true of our walk with God. Can you be more saved than you were the first day of your salvation? No. But can a person grow in salvation? Absolutely. It, like marriage, is a done deal and a daily development.

The blood is God's sacrifice for us.

The water is God's Spirit in us.

And we need both. John is very concerned that we know this. It's not enough to know *what* came forth; we must know *how they came forth:* "At once blood and water came out" (John 19:34). John doesn't emphasize one over the other. But, oh, how we do.

Some accept the blood but forget the water. They want to be saved but don't want to be changed.

Others accept the water but forget the blood. They are busy for Christ but never at peace in Christ.

What about you? Do you tend to lean one way or the other?

Do you feel so saved that you never serve? Are you so happy with the score of your team that you aren't getting out of the golf cart? If that is you, let me ask a question. Why does God have you on the course? Why didn't he beam you up the moment he saved you? The fact is, you and I are here for a reason, and that reason is to glorify God in our service.

Or is your tendency the opposite? Perhaps you always serve for fear of not being saved. Perhaps you don't trust your team. You're worried that a secret card exists on which your score is being written. Is that you? If so, know this: The blood of Jesus is enough to save you.

Engrave in your heart the announcement of John the Baptist.

Jesus is "the Lamb of God, who takes away the sin of the world" (John 1:29). The blood of Christ does not cover your sins, conceal your sins, postpone your sins, or diminish your sins. It takes away your sins, once and for all time.

Jesus allows your mistakes to be lost in his perfection. As the four of us golfers stood in the clubhouse to receive the award, the only ones who knew of the poverty of my game were my teammates, and they didn't tell.

When you and I stand in heaven to receive our prize, only one will know all of our sins, but he won't embarrass you—he has already forgiven them.

So enjoy the game, my friend; your prize is secure.

But you might ask the Teacher for some help with that swing.

12

"I WILL LOVE YOU FOREVER"

God's Promise in the Cross

For God so loved the world that
he gave his one and only Son,
that whoever believes in him shall
not perish but have eternal life.

JOHN 3:16 NIV

For our sake he made him to be sin who knew no sin,
so that in him we might become the righteousness of God.

2 CORINTHIANS 5:21 NRSV

But God demonstrates his own love for us in this:
While we were still sinners, Christ died for us.

ROMANS 5:8 NIV

This is love: not that we loved God,
but that he loved us and sent his Son
as an atoning sacrifice for our sins.

1 JOHN 4:10 NIV

People often ask me about the pronunciation of my last name. Is it Lu-KAY-doh or Lu-KAH-doh? Remember the verse in the song? "Some say po-tay-to; some say po-tah-to." The same can be sung about my name. "Some say Lu-KAY-doh; some say Lu-KAH-doh." For the record, we say "Lu-KAY-doh."

(Of course, we may be wrong. When Billy Graham came to San Antonio, he referred to me as Max Lu-KAH-doh. I guess if Billy Graham says Lu-KAH-doh, it must be Lu-KAH-doh.)

Confusion over the name has created some awkward moments. A notable one occurred when I visited one of our church members at his office. One of his coworkers spotted me. She'd been at our church and read a few of my books. "Max Lu-KAH-doh!" she exclaimed. "I've been wanting to meet you."

It seemed rude to correct her before I'd even met her, so I just smiled and said hello, thinking that would be the end of it. But it was just the beginning. She wanted me to meet a few friends. So down the hall we went, and with each introduction came a mispronunciation. "Sally, this is Max Lu-KAH-doh." "Joe, this is Max

Lu-KAH-doh." "Bob, this is Max Lu-KAH-doh." "Tom, this is Max Lu-KAH-doh." I would smile and cringe, unable to maneuver my way into the conversation to correct her. Besides, after half a dozen times, we reached the point of no return. Correcting her would have been too embarrassing. So I just kept my mouth shut.

But then I got caught. We finally met a fellow who beat her to the draw. "I'm so glad to see you," he said as we entered his office. "My wife and I visited your services last Sunday, and we left trying to figure out how you say your name. Is it Lu-KAY-doh or Lu-KAH-doh?"

I was trapped. Tell the truth, she'll be embarrassed. Lie, he will be misinformed. She needed mercy. He needed accuracy. I wanted to be kind with her and honest with him, but how could I be both? I couldn't. So I lied. For the first time in my entire life I answered, "Lu-KAH-doh, I pronounce the name, Lu-KAH-doh."

May my ancestors forgive me.

But the moment wasn't without its redeeming value. The situation provides a glimpse into the character of God. On an infinitely grander scale, God faces with humankind what I faced with the woman. How can he be both just and kind? How can he dispense truth and mercy? How can he redeem the sinner without endorsing the sin?

Can a holy God overlook our mistakes?

Can a kind God punish our mistakes?

From our perspective there are only two equally unappealing solutions. But from his perspective there is a third. It's called "the Cross of Christ."

The cross. Can you turn any direction without seeing one? Perched atop a chapel. Carved into a graveyard headstone.

Engraved in a ring or suspended on a chain. The cross is the universal symbol of Christianity. An odd choice, don't you think? Strange that a tool of torture would come to embody a movement of hope. The symbols of other faiths are more upbeat: the six-pointed star of David, the crescent moon of Islam, a lotus blossom for Buddhism. Yet a cross for Christianity? An instrument of execution?

Would you wear a tiny electric chair around your neck? Suspend a gold-plated hangman's noose on the wall? Would you print a picture of a firing squad on a business card? Yet we do so with the cross. Many even make the sign of the cross as they pray. Would we make the sign of, say, a guillotine? Instead of the triangular touch on the forehead and shoulders, how about a karate chop on the palm? Doesn't quite have the same feel, does it?

Why is the cross the symbol of our faith? To find the answer look no farther than the cross itself. Its design couldn't be simpler. One beam horizontal—the other vertical. One reaches out—like God's love. The other reaches up—as does God's holiness. One represents the width of his love; the other reflects the height of his holiness. The cross is the intersection. The cross is where God forgave his children without lowering his standards.

How could he do this? In a sentence: God put our sin on his Son and punished it there.

"God put on him the wrong who never did anything wrong, so we could be put right with God" (2 Cor. 5:21 MSG).

Or as rendered elsewhere: "Christ never sinned! But God treated him as a sinner, so that Christ could make us acceptable to God" (CEV).

Envision the moment. God on his throne. You on the earth.

And between you and God, suspended between you and heaven, is Christ on his cross. Your sins have been placed on Jesus. God, who punishes sin, releases his rightful wrath on your mistakes. Jesus receives the blow. Since Christ is between you and God, you don't. The sin is punished, but you are safe—safe in the shadow of the cross.

This is what God did, but why, why would he do it? Moral duty? Heavenly obligation? Paternal requirement? No. God is required to do nothing.

Besides, consider what he did. He gave his Son. His only Son. Would you do that? Would you offer the life of your child for someone else? I wouldn't. There are those for whom I would give my life. But ask me to make a list of those for whom I would kill my daughter? The sheet will be blank. I don't need a pencil. The list has no names.

But God's list contains the name of every person who ever lived. For this is the scope of his love. And this is the reason for the cross. He loves the world.

"For God so loved the world that he gave his only Son" (John 3:16 NLT).

As boldly as the center beam proclaims God's holiness, the crossbeam declares his love. And, oh, how wide his love reaches.

Aren't you glad the verse does not read:

"For God so loved the rich . . . "?

Or, "For God so loved the famous . . . "?

Or, "For God so loved the thin . . . "?

It doesn't. Nor does it state, "For God so loved the Europeans or Africans . . . " "the sober or successful . . . " "the young or the old . . . "

No, when we read John 3:16, we simply (and happily) read, "For God so loved the world."

How wide is God's love? Wide enough for the whole world. Are you included in the world? Then you are included in God's love.

It's nice to be included. You aren't always. Universities exclude you if you aren't smart enough. Businesses exclude you if you aren't qualified enough, and, sadly, some churches exclude you if you aren't good enough.

But though they may exclude you, Christ includes you. When asked to describe the width of his love, he stretched one hand to the right and the other to the left and had them nailed in that position so you would know he died loving you.

But isn't there a limit? Surely there has to be an end to this love. You'd think so, wouldn't you? But David the adulterer never found it. Paul the murderer never found it. Peter the liar never found it. When it came to life, they hit bottom. But when it came to God's love, they never did.

They, like you, found their names on God's list of love. And you can be certain that the One who put it there knows how to pronounce it.

13

"I CAN TURN YOUR TRAGEDY INTO TRIUMPH"

God's Promise in the Burial Clothing

Yet, O Lord, you are our Father;
we are the clay, and you are our potter;
we are all the work of your hand.

Isaiah 64:8 NRSV

I can do everything through him who gives me strength.

Philippians 4:13 NIV

I will be glad and rejoice in your love,
for you saw my affliction
and knew the anguish of my soul.
You have not handed me over to the enemy
but have set my feet in a spacious place.

Psalm 31:7–8 NIV

And the God of all grace,
who called you to his eternal glory in Christ,
after you have suffered a little while,
will himself restore you and make you strong,
firm and steadfast.

1 Peter 5:10 NIV

What do you say we have a chat about graveclothes? Sound like fun? Sound like a cheery topic? Hardly. Make a list of depressing subjects, and burial garments is somewhere between IRS audits and long-term dental care.

No one likes graveclothes. No one discusses graveclothes. Have you ever spiced up dinner-table chat with the question, "What are you planning to wear in your casket?" Have you ever seen a store specializing in burial garments? (If there is one, I have an advertising slogan to suggest: "Clothes to die for.")

Most folks don't discuss graveclothes.

The apostle John, however, was an exception. Ask him, and he'll tell you how he came to see burial garments as a symbol of triumph. He didn't always see them that way. A tangible reminder of the death of his best friend, Jesus, they used to seem like a symbol of tragedy. But on the first Easter Sunday, God took clothing of death and made it a symbol of life.

Could he do the same for you?

We all face tragedy. What's more, we've all received the symbols of tragedy. Yours might be a telegram from the war department, an ID bracelet from the hospital, a scar, or a court subpoena. We don't like these symbols, nor do we want these symbols. Like wrecked cars in a junkyard, they clutter up our hearts with memories of bad days.

Could God use such things for something good? How far can we go with verses like this one: "In everything God works for the good of those who love him" (Rom. 8:28)? Does "everything" include tumors and tests and tempers and terminations? John would answer yes. John would tell you that *God can turn any tragedy into a triumph, if only you will wait and watch.*

To prove his point, he would tell you about one Friday in particular.

> Later, Joseph from Arimathea asked Pilate if he could take the body of Jesus. (Joseph was a secret follower of Jesus, because he was afraid of some of the leaders.) Pilate gave his permission, so Joseph came and took Jesus' body away. Nicodemus, who earlier had come to Jesus at night, went with Joseph. He brought about seventy-five pounds of myrrh and aloes. These two men took Jesus' body and wrapped it with the spices in pieces of linen cloth, which is how they bury the dead. (John 19:38–40)

Reluctant during Christ's life but courageous at his death, Joseph and Nicodemus came to serve Jesus. They came to bury him. They ascended the hill bearing the burial clothing.

Pilate had given his permission.

Joseph of Arimathea had given a tomb.

Nicodemus had brought the spices and linens.

John states that Nicodemus brought seventy-five pounds of myrrh and aloes. The amount is worth noting, for such a quantity of burial ointments was typically used only for kings. John also comments on the linens because to him they were a picture of Friday's tragedy. As long as there were no graveclothes, as long as there was no tomb, as long as there was no coroner, there was hope. But the arrival of the hearse triggered the departure of any hope. And to this apostle, the graveclothes symbolized tragedy.

Could there have been a greater tragedy for John than a dead Jesus? Three years earlier John had turned his back on his career and cast his lot with this Nazarene carpenter. Earlier in the week John had enjoyed a ticker-tape parade as Jesus and the disciples entered Jerusalem. Oh, how quickly things had turned! The people who had called him king on Sunday called for his death the following Friday. These linens were a tangible reminder that his friend and his future were wrapped in cloth and sealed behind a rock.

John didn't know on that Friday what you and I now know. He didn't know that Friday's tragedy would be Sunday's triumph. John would later confess that he "did not yet understand from the Scriptures that Jesus must rise from the dead" (John 20:9).

That's why what he did on Saturday is so important.

We don't know anything about this day; we have no passage to read, no knowledge to share. All we know is this: When Sunday came, John was still present. When Mary Magdalene came looking for him, she found him.

Jesus was dead. The Master's body was lifeless. John's friend and future were buried. But John had not left. Why? Was he waiting for the resurrection? No. As far as he knew, the lips were forever silent and the hands forever still. He wasn't expecting a Sunday surprise. Then why was he here?

You'd think he would have left. Who was to say that the men who crucified Christ wouldn't come after him? The crowds were pleased with one crucifixion; the religious leaders might have called for more. Why didn't John get out of town?

Perhaps the answer was pragmatic; perhaps he was taking care of Jesus' mother. Or perhaps he didn't have anywhere else to go. Could be he didn't have any money or energy or direction . . . or all of the above.

Or maybe he lingered because he loved Jesus.

To others, Jesus was a miracle worker. To others, Jesus was a master teacher. To others, Jesus was the hope of Israel. But to John, he was all of these and more. To John, Jesus was a friend.

You don't abandon a friend—not even when that friend is dead. John stayed close to Jesus.

He had a habit of doing this. He was close to Jesus in the upper room. He was close to Jesus in the Garden of Gethsemane. He was at the foot of the cross at the crucifixion, and he was a quick walk from the tomb at the burial.

Did he understand Jesus? No.

Was he glad Jesus did what he did? No.

But did he leave Jesus? No.

What about you? When you're in John's position, what do you do? When it's Saturday in your life, how do you react? When you are somewhere between yesterday's tragedy and tomorrow's triumph, what do you do? Do you leave God—or do you linger near him?

John chose to linger. And because he lingered on Saturday, he was around on Sunday to see the miracle.

> Mary said, "They have taken the Lord out of the tomb, and we don't know where they have put him."
>
> So Peter and the other follower started for the tomb. They were both running, but the other follower ran faster than Peter and reached the tomb first. He bent down and looked in and saw the strips of linen cloth lying there, but he did not go in. Then following him, Simon Peter arrived and went into the tomb and saw the strips of linen lying there. He also saw the cloth that had been around Jesus' head, which was folded up and laid in a different place from the strips of linen. Then the other follower, who had reached the tomb first, also went in. He saw and believed. (John 20:2–8)

Very early on Sunday morning Peter and John were given the news: "Jesus' body is missing!" Mary was urgent, both with her announcement and her opinion. She thought Jesus' enemies had taken his body away. Instantly the two disciples hurried to the sepulcher, John outrunning Peter and arriving first. What he saw so stunned him he froze at the entrance.

What did he see? "Strips of linen cloth." He saw "the cloth that had been around Jesus' head . . . folded up and laid in a different place from the strips of linen." He saw "cloth lying."

The original Greek provides helpful insight here. John employs a term that means "rolled up,"[1] "still in their folds."[2] These burial wraps had not been ripped off and thrown down. They were still in their original state! The linens were undisturbed. The graveclothes were still rolled and folded.

How could this be?

If friends had removed the body, would they not have taken the clothes with it?

If foes had taken the body, would they not have done the same?

If not, if for some reason friends or foes had unwrapped the body, would they have been so careful as to dispose of the clothing in such an orderly fashion? Of course not!

But if neither friend nor foe took the body, who did?

This was John's question, and this question led to John's discovery. "He saw and believed" (John 20:8).

Through the rags of death, John saw the power of life. Odd, don't you think, that God would use something as sad as a burial wrap to change a life?

But God is given to such practices:

In his hand empty wine jugs at a wedding become a symbol of power.

The coin of a widow becomes a symbol of generosity.

A crude manger in Bethlehem is his symbol of devotion.

And a tool of death is a symbol of his love.

Should we be surprised that he takes the wrappings of death and makes them the picture of life?

Which takes us back to the question. Could God do something similar in your life? Could he take what today is a token of tragedy and turn it into a symbol of triumph?

He did for my friend Rafael Rosales. Rafael is a minister in El Salvador. The Salvadoran guerrillas viewed him as an enemy of their movement and tried to kill him. Left to die in a burning automobile, Rafael escaped the car and the country. But he couldn't escape the memories. The scars would not let him.

Every glance in the mirror reminded him of his tormentors' cruelty. He might have never recovered had the Lord not spoken to his heart. "They did the same to me" he heard his Savior say. And as God ministered to Rafael, Rafael began to see his scars differently. Rather than serve as a reminder of his own pain, they became a picture of his Savior's sacrifice. In time he was able to forgive his attackers. During the very week that I write these words, he is visiting his country, looking for a place to plant a new church.

Could such a change happen to you? I have no doubt. You simply need to do what John did. Don't leave. Hang around.

Remember the second half of the passage. "God works for the good of *those who love him*" (Rom. 8:28, italics mine). That's how John felt about Jesus. He loved him. He didn't understand him or always agree with him, but he loved him.

And because he loved him, he stayed near him.

The Bible says that "in everything God works for the good of those who love him." Before we close this chapter, do this simple exercise. Remove the word *everything,* and replace it with the symbol of your tragedy. For the apostle John, the verse would read: "In *burial clothing* God works for the good of those who love him." For Rafael it would read: "In *scars* God works for the good of those who love him."

How would Romans 8:28 read in your life?

In hospital stays God works for the good.

In divorce papers God works for the good.

In a prison term God works for the good.

If God can change John's life through a tragedy, could it be he will use a tragedy to change yours?

As hard as it may be to believe, you could be only a Saturday away from a resurrection. You could be only hours from that precious prayer of a changed heart, "God, did you do this for me?"

14

"I HAVE WON THE VICTORY"

God's Promise in the Empty Tomb

With the cross, [God] won the victory.

COLOSSIANS 2:15

On the first Easter morning . . . the smothering silence
that insulates the domain of the dead from the
world of the living was suddenly shattered.

GILBERT BILEZIKIAN

But now in a single victorious stroke of Life,
all three—sin, guilt, death—are gone,
the gift of our Master, Jesus Christ. Thank God!

1 CORINTHIANS 15:57 MSG

But thanks be to God,
who always leads us in victory through Christ.

2 CORINTHIANS 2:14

His Birth

The words of King Herod when told of the birth of Jesus. "Kill him. There is room for only one king in this corner of the world."

The number of religious leaders who believed a messiah had been born in Bethlehem. Zero.

The type of people who did. Some stargazers, night-shift shepherds, and a couple of newlyweds who claimed to have more experience giving birth than having sex.

The reward given to Joseph and Mary for bringing God into the world. Two years in exile, learning Egyptian.

This was the beginning of the Christian movement. (And these were the calm years.)

His Ministry

The word on the streets of Jesus' hometown when he claimed to be sent from God. Weird family. Have you seen his cousin?

The reaction of the hometown folks. Stone him.

The opinion of his brothers. Lock him up.

The number of disciples Jesus recruited. Seventy.

The number of disciples who defended him to the authorities. Zero.

The assessment of Jesus' followers as found in the Jerusalem editorial page. A group of unemployed ne'er-do-wells recruited off the shipping docks and out of the red-light districts.

The number of lepers and blind and lame people Jesus healed. Too many to count.

The number of healed lepers and blind and lame people who defended Jesus on the day of his death. Zero.

His Execution

The popular opinion regarding Jesus before he cleansed the Temple. See if he'll run for office.

The popular opinion regarding Jesus after he cleansed the Temple. Let's see how fast he can run.

The decision of the Jewish council. Three spikes and a spear.

The talk on the streets of Jerusalem after Jesus died. He should've stayed in the furniture business.

The number of times Jesus prophesied that he would come back to life three days after his death. Three.

The number of apostles who heard the prophecy. All of them.

The number of apostles who waited at the tomb to see if he would do what he said. Zero.

The number of his followers who believed in the resurrection before it occurred. You do the math.

The odds a street-corner bookie would've given the day after the crucifixion on the possibility that Jesus' name would be known in the year 2000. "I'll give you better odds that he'll rise from the dead."

His Movement

The official response of the Jewish leaders to the rumors of the resurrection. Of course they say he's alive. They have to. What else can they say?

The actual response of the Jewish leaders to the resurrection of Jesus. "A great number of the Jewish priests believed and obeyed" (Acts 6:7).

The decision of the Jewish leaders about the church. "If their plan comes from human authority, it will fail. But if it is from God, you will not be able to stop them" (Acts 5:38–39).

The response of the church. "The number of followers was growing" (Acts 6:1).

The official response of the Jewish leaders to the conversion of Saul. Good riddance to the former Pharisee. Won't be months before he is in jail, and then what will he do? Write letters?

What Saul, turned Paul, understood that his former colleagues didn't. "God gave [Jesus] as a way to forgive sin" (Rom. 3:25).

The Movement Continues

The belief of French philosopher Voltaire. The Bible and Christianity would pass within a hundred years. He died in 1778. The movement continues.

The pronouncement of Friedrich Nietzsche in 1882. "God is dead." The dawn of science, he believed, would be the doom of faith. Science has dawned; the movement continues.

The way a Communist dictionary defined the Bible. "It is a collection of fantastic legends without any scientific support." Communism is diminishing; the movement continues.

The discovery made by every person who has tried to bury the faith. The same as the one made by those who tried to bury its Founder: He won't stay in the tomb.

The facts. The movement has never been stronger. Over one billion Catholics and nearly as many Protestants.

The question. How do we explain it? Jesus was a backwater peasant. He never wrote a book, never held an office. He never journeyed more than two hundred miles from his hometown. Friends left him. One betrayed him. Those he helped forgot him. Prior to his death they abandoned him. But after his death they couldn't resist him. What made the difference?

The answer. His death and resurrection.

For when he died, so did your sin.

And when he rose, so did your hope.

For when he rose, your grave was changed from a final residence to temporary housing.

The reason he did it. The face in your mirror.

The verdict after two millenniums. Herod was right: there is room for only one King.

15

WHAT WILL YOU LEAVE AT THE CROSS?

Trust in the LORD with all your heart
and lean not on your own understanding;
in all your ways acknowledge him,
and he will make your paths straight.

PROVERBS 3:5–6 NIV

Cast all your anxiety on him because he cares for you.

1 PETER 5:7 NIV

No one can well perceive the power of faith
unless he feels it by experience in his heart.

JOHN CALVIN

You yourself in your own conscience must feel Christ himself.
You must experience unshakably that it is God's Word,
even though the whole world should dispute it.
As long as you do not have this feeling,
you have certainly not yet tasted of God's Word.

MARTIN LUTHER

The hill is quiet now. Not still but quiet. For the first time all day there is no noise. The clamor began to subside when the darkness—that puzzling midday darkness—fell. Like water douses a fire, the shadows doused the ridicule. No more taunts. No more jokes. No more jesting. And, in time, no more mockers. One by one the onlookers turned and began the descent.

That is, all the onlookers except you and me. We did not leave. We came to learn. And so we lingered in the semidarkness and listened. We listened to the soldiers cursing, the passersby questioning, and the women weeping. But most of all, we listened to the trio of dying men groaning. Hoarse, guttural, thirsty groans. They groaned with each rolling of the head and each pivot of the legs.

But as the minutes became hours, these groans diminished. The three seemed dead. Were it not for the belabored breathing, you would have thought they were.

Then he screamed. As if someone had yanked his hair, the back of his head slammed against the sign that bore his name, and he screamed. Like a dagger cuts the curtain, his scream cut the dark.

Standing as straight as the nails would permit, he cried as one calling for a lost friend, *"Eloi!"*

His voice was raspy, scratchy. Reflections of the torch flame danced in his wide eyes. "My God!"

Ignoring the volcano of erupting pain, he pushed upward until his shoulders were higher than his nailed hands. "Why have you forsaken me?"

The soldiers stared. The weeping of the women ceased. One of the Pharisees sneered sarcastically, "He's calling Elijah."

No one laughed.

He'd shouted a question to the heavens, and you half expected heaven to shout one in return.

And apparently it did. For the face of Jesus softened, and an afternoon dawn broke as he spoke a final time. "It is finished. Father, into your hands I commit my spirit."

As he gave his final breath, the earth gave a sudden stir. A rock rolled, and a soldier stumbled. Then, as suddenly as the silence was broken, the silence returned.

And now all is quiet. The mocking has ceased. There is no one to mock.

The soldiers are busy with the business of cleaning up the dead. Two men have come. Dressed well and meaning well, they are given the body of Jesus.

And we are left with the relics of his death.

Three nails in a bin.

Three cross-shaped shadows.

A braided crown with scarlet tips.

Bizarre, isn't it? The thought that this blood is not man's blood but God's?

Crazy, isn't it? To think that these nails held your sins to a cross?

Absurd, don't you agree? That a scoundrel's prayer was offered and answered? Or more absurd that another scoundrel offered no prayer at all?

Absurdities and ironies. The hill of Calvary is nothing if not both.

We would have scripted the moment differently. Ask us how a God should redeem his world, and we will show you! White horses, flashing swords. Evil flat on his back. God on his throne.

But God on a cross?

A split-lipped, puffy-eyed, blood-masked God on a cross?

Sponge thrust in his face?

Spear plunged in his side?

Dice tossed at his feet?

No, we wouldn't have written the drama of redemption this way. But, then again, we weren't asked to. These players and props were heaven picked and God ordained. We were not asked to design the hour.

But we have been asked to respond to it. In order for the cross of Christ to be the cross of your life, you and I need to bring something to the hill.

We have seen what Jesus brought. With scarred hands he offered forgiveness. Through torn skin he promised acceptance. He took the path to take us home. He wore our garment to give us his own. We have seen the gifts he brought.

Now we ask, what will we bring?

We aren't asked to paint the sign or carry the nails. We aren't asked to wear the spit or bear the crown. But we are asked to walk the path and leave something at the cross.

We don't have to, of course. Many don't.

Many have done what we have done: More minds than ours have read about the cross; better minds than mine have written about it. Many have pondered what Christ left; fewer have pondered what we must leave.

May I urge you to leave something at the cross? You can observe the cross and analyze the cross. You can read about it, even pray to it. But until you leave something there, you haven't embraced the cross.

You've seen what Christ left. Won't you leave something as well? Why don't you start with your *bad moments?*

Those bad habits? Leave them at the cross. Your selfish moods and white lies? Give them to God. Your binges and bigotries? God wants them all. Every flop, every failure. He wants every single one. Why? Because he knows we can't live with them.

I grew up playing football in the empty field next to our house. Many a Sunday afternoon was spent imitating Don Meredith or Bob Hayes or Johnny Unitas. (Didn't have to imitate Joe Namath. Most of the girls thought I looked like him already.)

Empty fields in West Texas have grass burrs. Grass burrs hurt. You can't play football without falling, and you can't fall in a West Texas field without getting stuck.

More times than I can remember I pulled myself out of a sticker patch so hopelessly covered that I had to have help. Kids don't rely on other kids to pull out grass burrs. You need someone with skill. I would limp to the house so my dad could pluck out the stickers—one by painful one.

I wasn't too bright, but I knew this: If I wanted to get back into the game, I needed to get rid of those stickers.

Every mistake in life is like a grass burr. You can't live without falling, and you can't fall without getting stuck. But guess what? We aren't always as smart as young ballplayers. We sometimes try to get back into the game without dealing with the stickers. It's as if we don't want anyone to know we fell, so we pretend we never did. Consequently, we live in pain. We can't walk well, sleep well, rest well. And, oh, are we touchy.

Does God want us to live like that? No way. Listen to his promise: "This is my commitment to my people: removal of their sins" (Rom. 11:27 MSG).

God does more than forgive our mistakes; he removes them! We simply have to take them to him.

He not only wants the mistakes we've made. He wants the ones we are making! Are you making some? Are you drinking too much? Are you cheating at work or cheating at marriage? Are you mismanaging money? Are you mismanaging your life?

If so, don't pretend nothing is wrong. Don't pretend you don't fall. Don't try to get back in the game. Go first to God. The first step after a stumble must be in the direction of the cross. "If we confess our sins to God, he can always be trusted to forgive us and take our sins away" (1 John 1:9 CEV).

What can you leave at the cross? Start with your bad moments. And while you are there, give God your *mad moments*.

Do you remember the story about the man who was bitten by the dog? When he learned the dog had rabies, he began making a list. The doctor told him there was no need to make a will, that rabies could be cured. "Oh, I'm not making a will," he replied. "I'm making a list of all the people I want to bite."

Couldn't we all make such a list? You've already learned,

haven't you, that friends aren't always friendly? Neighbors aren't always neighborly? Some workers never work, and some bosses are always bossy?

You've already learned, haven't you, that a promise made is not always a promise kept? Just because someone is called your dad, that doesn't mean he will act like your dad. Even though they said "yes" on the altar, they may say "no" in the marriage.

You've already learned, haven't you, that we tend to fight back? To bite back? To keep lists and snarl lips and growl at people we don't like?

God wants your list. He inspired one servant to write, "Love does not keep a record of wrongs" (1 Cor. 13:5 TEV). He wants us to leave the list at the cross.

Not easy.

"Just look what they did to me!" we defy and point to our hurts.

"Just look what I did for you," he reminds and points to the cross.

Paul said it this way: "If someone does wrong to you, forgive that person because the Lord forgave you" (Col. 3:13).

You and I are commanded—not urged, *commanded*—to keep no list of wrongs.

Besides, do you really want to keep one? Do you really want to catalog all your mistreatments? Do you really want to growl and snap your way through life? God doesn't want you to either. Give up your sins before they infect you and your bitterness before it incites you, and give God your anxiety before it inhibits you. Give God your *anxious moments*.

A man told his psychologist that his anxieties were disturbing his dreams. Some nights he dreamed he was a pup tent; other nights he dreamed he was a tepee. The doctor quickly analyzed the situation and replied, "I know your problem. You're too tense."[1]

Most of us are. We parents have it especially tough. My daughters are at that age when they are starting to drive. It seems like just yesterday I was teaching them to walk, and now I'm putting them behind a steering wheel. It's a scary thought. I'm thinking of making a special bumper sticker for Jenna's car that reads, "How am I driving? 1-800-CALL-DAD."

What do we do with these worries? Take your anxieties to the cross—literally. Next time you're worried about your health or house or finances or flights, take a mental trip up the hill. Spend a few moments looking again at the pieces of passion.

Run your thumb over the tip of the spear. Balance a spike in the palm of your hand. Read the wooden sign written in your own language. And as you do, touch the velvet dirt, moist with the blood of God.

Blood he bled for you.

The spear he took for you.

The nails he felt for you.

The sign he left for you.

He did all of this for you. Knowing this, knowing all he did for you there, don't you think he'll look out for you here?

Or as Paul wrote, "God did not keep back his own Son, but he gave him for us. If God did this, won't he freely give us everything else?" (Rom. 8:32 CEV).

---

[1]Get it? Too tense. Two tents. *Why are you groaning?*

Do yourself a favor; take your anxious moments to the cross. Leave them there with your bad moments, your mad moments, and your anxious moments. And may I suggest one more? Your *final moment*.

Barring the return of Christ first, you and I will have one. A final moment. A final breath. A final widening of the eyes and beating of the heart. In a split second you'll leave what you know and enter what you don't.

That's what bothers us. Death is the great unknown. We're always a bit skittish about the unknown.

Sara certainly was. Denalyn and I thought it was a great idea. We would kidnap the girls from school and take them on a weekend trip. We made reservations at a hotel and cleared the trip with their teachers but kept it a secret from our girls. When we showed up at Sara's fourth grade classroom on Friday afternoon, we thought she'd be thrilled. She wasn't. She was afraid. She didn't want to leave!

As we left, I assured her nothing was wrong. We had come to take her to a fun place. Didn't work. By the time we got to the car, she was crying. She was confused. She didn't like the interruption.

Nor do we. God promises to come at an unexpected hour and take us from the gray world we know to a golden world we don't. But since we don't, we aren't sure we want to go. We even get upset at the thought of his coming.

For that reason God wants us to do what Sara finally did—trust her father. "Don't let your hearts be troubled," he urged. "I will come back and take you to be with me so that you may be where I am" (John 14:1, 3).

By the way, in a short time Sara relaxed and enjoyed the trip. In fact, she didn't want to come back. You won't want to either.

Troubled about your final moments? Leave them at the foot of the cross.

Leave them there with your bad moments, mad moments, and anxious moments.

About this time someone is thinking, "You know, Max, if I leave all those moments at the cross, I won't have any moments left but good ones."

Well, what do you know? I guess you won't.

FINAL WORDS

There is nothing impressive about the stationery. No embossed letters. No watermark. No heavy stock paper. No logo. Just a sheet of yellow legal-pad paper, the top of which is jagged from the tear.

There is nothing impressive about the handwriting. There used to be. As a child, I tried to imitate it. But you wouldn't want to imitate this penmanship; you'd be hard-pressed to decipher it. Angled lines. Irregular letters and inconsistent spacing.

But it was the best my father could do. Lou Gehrig's disease had so weakened his hands he could scarcely bring a fork to his mouth, much less write words on a page. Imagine writing with all your fingers wrapped around the pen, and you're close to understanding his challenge.

It was the final letter he wrote us. The ALS and cold weather had nearly killed him. Denalyn and I had rushed home from Brazil and spent a month eating hospital food and taking shifts at his bedside. He rebounded, however, so we returned to South America. A day or so after arriving, we received this letter.

January 19, 1984

Dear Max and Denalyn,

We were glad you all made it home OK. Now settle down and go to work. We enjoyed your trip to no end. Even your spending the nights with me.

MAX, YOU AND DENALYN ALWAYS STICK TOGETHER, WHATEVER HAPPENS.

Well, there is no need of me scribbling. I think you know how much I love you both. You all just live good Christian lives and FEAR GOD.

I hope to see you all again on earth—if not, I will in heaven.

Lots of love,

Dad

I've envisioned my father writing those words. Propped up in a hospital bed, pen in hand, pad on lap. Thinking this would be his final message. Do you suppose he chose his words carefully? Of course he did.

Can you envision trying to do the same? Can you imagine your final message to those you love? Your last words with a child or spouse?

What would you say? How would you say it?

Even if you can't answer the first question, you can answer the second. How would you say your final words? Deliberately. Carefully. Wouldn't you go as Monet to a palette—searching for, not just the right color, but the perfect shade, the exact hue? Most of us have only one chance to make our last statement.

That's all Jesus was given. Knowing his last deeds would be forever pondered, don't you think he chose them carefully?

Deliberately? Of course he did. There were no accidents that day. Jesus' last moments were not left up to chance. God chose the path; he selected the nails. Our Lord planted the trio of crosses and painted the sign. God was never more sovereign than in the details of the death of his Son. As deliberately as my father wrote the letter, so your Father left this message:

"I did it for you. I did it all for you."

Notes

Chapter 2: "I Will Bear Your Dark Side"

1. Michel de Montaigne, *Quote Unquote,* quoted in Lloyd Cory ed., (Wheaton Ill.: Victor Books, 1977), 297.

Chapter 5: "I Will Speak to You in Your Language"

1. Isabel McHugh and Florence McHugh, trans., *The Trial of Jesus: The Jewish and Roman Proceedings against Jesus Christ Described and Assessed from the Oldest Accounts* by Josef Blinzler (Westminster, Md.: The Newman Press, 1959), 103.
2. George Sayer, *Jack: A Life of C. S. Lewis* (Wheaton, Ill.: Crossway Books, 1994), 222.
3. McHugh and McHugh, *The Trial of Jesus,* 104.

Chapter 6: "I Will Let You Choose"

1. Paul Aurandt, *Paul Harvey's the Rest of the Story* (New York: Bantam Press, 1977), 47.

Chapter 7: "I Will Not Abandon You"

1. "If you, then, though you are evil, know how to give good gifts to your children, how much more will your Father in heaven give good gifts to those who ask him!" (Matt. 7:11 NIV).

2. Frank Stagg, *New Testament Theology* (Nashville: Broadman Press, 1962), 102.

Chapter 8: "I Will Give You My Robe"

1. McHugh and McHugh, *The Trial of Jesus,* 1038.

Chapter 9: "I Invite You into My Presence"

1. *Illustrated Bible Dictionary*, vol. 3 (Wheaton, Ill.: Tyndale House, 1980), 1525.

Chapter 10: "I Understand Your Pain"

1. William Hendriksen, *Exposition of the Gospel According to John,* of *New Testament Commentary* (Grand Rapids: Baker Book House, 1953), 431.
2. Pss. 22:15; 69:21.

Chapter 13: "I Can Turn Your Tragedy into Triumph"

1. Arthur W. Pink, *Exposition of the Gospel of John* (Grand Rapids: Zondervan, 1975), 1077.
2. William Barclay, *The Gospel of John,* vol. 2, rev. ed. (Philadelphia: Westminster Press, 1975), 267.

STUDY GUIDE

Compiled by Steve Halliday

1

You Did This for Me?

Nailing It Down

A. "Oh, the things we do to give gifts to those we love."
   1. Describe some of the memorable gifts you have received from a loved one.
   2. Describe a specially chosen gift for someone you love. What made it unique?
   3. Why do we go to such great lengths to delight those we love?

B. "We are at our best when we are giving. In fact, we are most like God when we are giving."
   1. What do you think Max means by this statement?
   2. Do you agree with him? Why or why not?
   3. How can you be like God in your giving *this week?*

C. "Have you ever wondered why God gives so much? We could exist on far less. He could have left the world flat and gray; we wouldn't have known the difference. But he didn't."
   1. Why do you think God gives so much?
   2. What aspects of God's creation most delight your heart?

3. Why is salvation the most amazing gift?

D. "Every gift reveals God's love . . . but no gift reveals his love more than the gifts of the cross."
1. What gifts have you received from God? What do they mean to you?

2. List several "gifts of the cross" and explain how each reveals God's love.

3. What gift of the cross speaks most profoundly to your heart? Why?

Glimpsing God's Heart

A. Read Romans 6:23.
1. What gift from God is mentioned here?

2. How does one receive this gift?

3. What is Jesus' connection to this gift?

B. Read 2 Corinthians 9:15.
1. What gift from God is mentioned here?

2. Why is this gift called "indescribable" (NIV)?

3. How are we to respond to this gift? Why?

C. Read 1 Peter 1:3–5.

1. What gift from God is described here?

2. Where is this gift kept? Why is it kept there?

3. When will we receive this gift? How can we be sure of this?

D. Read James 1:17–18.

1. Where do all good gifts come from?

2. What did God choose to do for us? How did he accomplish this?

3. Why did God choose to do this? What did he want to accomplish?

E. Read Matthew 7:9–11.

1. What point does this passage make?

2. What promise is made here? How is that promise meant to sustain us?

Making a Choice

A. If we are "most like God when we are giving," how can you "be like God" this week? Whom can you bless with an unexpected gift? What kind of gift should this be? When can you give it? How can you present it to make the moment extraspecial? Plan the details of your gift giving, and then carry it out before the end of this week.

B. Set aside at least fifteen minutes to thank God for all of his gifts to you. Before you begin, make a list of the gifts for which you are especially grateful. Conclude your prayer time with a special focus on God's gift of salvation. Try hard not to bring up any requests during this holy time, but instead pour out your heart in thanksgiving to God for all his rich gifts to you.

2

"I Will Bear Your Dark Side"

Nailing It Down

A. "Ever since the curse, we've been different. Beastly. Ugly. Defiant. Angry. We do things we know we shouldn't do and wonder why we did them."

1. To what event does Max refer when he refers to "the curse"? How did this event change everything?

2. In what kinds of situations is your own "fallen nature" most likely to surface?

3. If you feel comfortable doing so, describe the last time you did something you knew you shouldn't do, only to wonder later why you did it.

B. "The soldiers felt big by making Christ look small. Ever done that? Maybe you've never spit on anyone, but have you gossiped? Slandered? Have you ever raised your hand in anger or rolled your eyes in arrogance?"

1. Describe a time when you saw someone trying to feel big by making someone else look small.

2. Answer Max's questions. Why did you act in this way? What happened when you did so?

3. How did those experiences help you grow and change?

C. "It is not that we *can't* do good. We do. It's just that we can't keep from doing bad. In theological terms, we are 'totally depraved.' Though made in God's image, we have fallen. We're corrupt at the core. The very center of our being is selfish and perverse."

1. In your own terms, how would you define "total depravity"?

2. Do you believe it's impossible for us to keep from doing bad? Explain.

3. Describe the first time you saw in yourself that "the very center of our being is selfish and perverse."

D. "A pig might look at his trough partners and announce, 'I'm just as clean as everyone else.' Compared to humans, however, that pig needs help. Compared to God, we humans need the same. The standard for sinlessness isn't found at the pig troughs of earth but at the throne of heaven. God, himself, is the standard."

1. Why do we tend to compare ourselves with others around us? What's wrong with this comparison?

2. In what way is God the standard for our behavior?

3. What kind of help for our propensity to sin can we expect to receive from the "throne of heaven"? Explain.

E. "In the Bible, the Beauty . . . becomes the beast so the beast can become the beauty. Jesus changes places with us."
   1. Who is "the Beauty"? Who is "the beast"?

   2. What does Max mean by "Jesus changes places with us"?

   3. What is "the beast" in you? (What beastly traits must God forgive in you?)

Glimpsing God's Heart

A. Read Psalms 36:1; 51:5; Jeremiah 17:9; Romans 3:10, 23; Ephesians 2:3.
   1. What claim do all these verses make about us?

   2. How does this affect our relationship with God? With each other?

   3. In what way do these verses paint us as "beastly"?

B. Read Jeremiah 13:23 and Romans 8:7.
   1. What hope for change do any of us have by relying on our own resources? Explain.

   2. What does it mean to have a mind "controlled by the sinful self"? What results from this condition?

C. Read Romans 6:23; Hebrews 12:14; Proverbs 10:16.
   1. What are "the wages of sin" (NIV)?

2. What is promised to those who do not have a holy life?

3. With what does God pay "evil people"?

D. Read Galatians 3:13–14.
1. What did Jesus do for us?

2. Why did he do this?

3. What did he accomplish by doing this?

Making a Choice

A. Some people think that the label "totally depraved" sounds too harsh. To these folks, Max issues the following challenge: "For the next twenty-four hours lead a sinless life." Do an experiment. One day this week take up Max's challenge (and take along a notebook to record what happens).

B. Get by yourself in a quiet part of your house, sit down, close your eyes, and try to put yourself in Jesus' place during the awful moments when the soldiers abused him. Imagine the hard slaps across your mouth, the cruel mocking and jeering, the spittle dripping down your cheeks. What do you feel? What are you thinking? Remember: Jesus did all this not only for the soldiers who beat him, but for *you*. Be sure to give him thanks for choosing to suffer such dreadful abuse *for you*.

3

"I Loved You Enough to Become One of You"

Nailing It Down

A. "When God entered time and became a man, he who was boundless became bound. Imprisoned in flesh. Restricted by weary-prone muscles and eyelids. For more than three decades, his once limitless reach would be limited to the stretch of an arm, his speed checked to the pace of human feet."

1. What do you think would be the hardest part about exchanging boundlessness for being bound? Why?

2. Is it easy for you to think of Jesus as completely human (although without sin)? Explain.

3. Why would Jesus exchange the limitless condition he knew in heaven for the severe limits of earth?

B. "Throughout Scripture thorns symbolize, not sin, but the consequence of sin. Remember Eden? After Adam and Eve sinned, God cursed the land. . . . Brambles on earth are the product of sin in the heart."

1. How are thorns an appropriate symbol for the consequences of sin?

2. What "thorns" have you experienced in your life? Explain.

3. Why do you think the thorns placed on Jesus' head were called a "crown"? Why not a "wreath" or a "circle"?

C. "Jesus never knew the fruits of sin . . . until he became sin for us. And when he did, all the emotions of sin tumbled in on him like shadows in a forest. He felt anxious, guilty, and alone."

1. Describe some of the "emotions of sin" that you have felt.

2. How did sin make Jesus feel "anxious"? "Guilty"? "Alone"?

3. Why does sin create these painful emotions in us?

D. "Want to know the coolest thing about the One who gave up the crown of heaven for a crown of thorns? He did it for you. Just for you."

1. Try to describe how you feel, knowing that Jesus gave up the crown of heaven for a crown of thorns "just for you."

2. How do you know this is true? Explain.

Glimpsing God's Heart

A. Read John 19:2–3.

1. What did the soldiers do in this passage?

2. Why did they do it? What did they want to accomplish?

3. Why did Jesus stand for this sort of brutal treatment?

B. Read Colossians 1:19 and John 1:14.

1. What do these passages teach us about Jesus? What do these scriptures reveal about his humanity? His holiness?

2. What does it mean that Jesus was full of "grace" and "truth"?

C. Read 1 Peter 1:18–20.

1. In what sense are we "bought"?

2. What was our "purchase price"?

3. Why was Christ "shown to the world"?

D. Read Matthew 27:45–46.

1. What is the significance of the "darkness" described in this passage?

2. Why did Jesus cry out "in a loud voice"?

3. Why *had* God forsaken Jesus at this point?

4. Read Psalm 22 to gain a fuller understanding of Jesus' awful cry.

Making a Choice

A. Do a little "field work" this week. If season and weather permit, visit a nearby open field where you can get "up close and personal" with some thorns. Look for several kinds of thorns and gather a few. Notice their texture; feel their sharp edges. Imagine their tearing the scalp of the Savior. Try to gain a new appreciation for and a fresh insight into the lengths Christ was willing to go for you.

B. For a week, meditate on the crown of thorns Jesus wore, and keep a diary of any new insights you gain. You might share your meditations with a friend.

4

"I Forgive You"

Nailing It Down

A. "Would you like anyone to see the list of your weaknesses? Would you like them made public? How would you feel if they were posted high so that everyone, including Christ himself, could see?"
   1. Answer each of Max's questions.

   2. If this list of personal weaknesses were posted at your front door, how do you think visitors would react?

B. "Dangling from the cross is an itemized catalog of your sins. The bad decisions from last year. The bad attitudes from last week. There, in broad daylight for all of heaven to see, is a list of your mistakes."
   1. Do you think such a list actually exists? Explain.

   2. If such a list exists, how does that make you feel? Explain.

C. "The list God has made, however, cannot be read. The words can't be deciphered. The mistakes are covered. The sins are hidden. Those at the top are hidden by his hand; those down the list are covered by his blood."
   1. How does God cover your "list"?

2. How does it make you feel to know that this list is hidden and covered? Why?

D. "What kept him from resisting? This warrant, this tabulation of your failures. He knew the price of those sins was death. He knew the source of those sins was you, and since he couldn't bear the thought of eternity without you, he chose the nails."
   1. How did a tabulation of your failures keep Jesus from resisting the nails?

   2. Why is death the price of sin? Isn't that a little harsh?

   3. How does it make you feel that Jesus "couldn't bear the thought of eternity without you"?

Glimpsing God's Heart

A. Read Acts 2:22–24.
   1. In this passage, how does Peter describe Christ's ministry?
   2. Who handed Christ over to "wicked men" (NIV), according to Peter?

   3. What part did nails play in this event?

B. Read Colossians 2:13–14.
   1. What did God do for us?

   2. How did he accomplish this?

3. What kind of "debt" did God cancel? How was this accomplished?

4. How was our "record" of sin "nailed" to the cross?

C. Read Romans 3:22–25.

1. What does it mean to "fall short of the glory of God" (NIV)? Who has done this?

2. What does it mean to be "justified" (NIV)? How was this accomplished?

3. How does faith access the work of Christ on the cross?

4. Have you put your faith in the work of Christ? If so, describe how. If not, why not?

Making a Choice

A. To get a small impression of the enormity of what God has forgiven you in Christ, write down every sin that you committed in the last two days. Try to leave nothing out—the harsh words, the uncaring attitudes, the selfish actions. Don't rush over the process; try to compile as thorough an inventory as possible. After you are satisfied that you have listed everything you can remember, tear up the list. And thank God that he has forgiven you of "all your sins"!

B. One way to thank God for his infinite forgiveness is to follow his example and forgive those who have wronged us. Is there someone in your life you need to forgive? Someone who needs to hear you say, "I forgive you"? Don't delay; approach that individual and forgive him or her with the love of Christ.

5

"I Will Speak to You in Your Language"

Nailing It Down

A. "Wise is the man who learns the nonverbal language of his wife, who notes the nods and discerns the gestures. It's not just what is said, but how. It's not just how, but when. It's not just when, but where. Good husbanding is good decoding. You've got to read the signs."

1. If you are married, do you know the "nonverbal language" of your spouse? If so, describe it. How did you learn it?

2. Describe your own nonverbal language. What gestures mean "keep away"? What tone means "you've hurt me"?

B. "Could it be that this piece of wood is a picture of God's devotion? A symbol of his passion to tell the world about his Son? A reminder that God will do whatever it takes to share with you the message of this sign?"

1. How was the sign on the cross a "picture of God's devotion"?

2. How did the sign tell the world about Jesus? What did it say?

3. How has God done "whatever it takes" to share with you his love?

C. "The sign reveals two truths about God's desire to reach the world:
- There is no person he will not use.
- There is no language he will not speak."

1. What person did God use to reach you?

2. What language did God use to reach you?

3. How might God want to use you to reach someone else? What "language" might you have to speak to these individuals?

D. "Pilate had intended the sign to threaten and mock the Jews. But God had another purpose . . . Pilate was God's instrument for spreading the gospel."

1. How had Pilate intended to threaten and mock the Jews through this sign?

2. How was Pilate God's instrument for spreading the gospel?

3. Describe some incident from your life in which God used an evil human intention to accomplish his holy will.

E. "What language is God speaking to you?
- the language of abundance
- the language of need

- the language of affliction"

1. What does Max mean by the "language of abundance"?

2. Explain the "language of need."

3. How would you define the "language of affliction"?

4. How does God most often seem to speak to you? Explain.

Glimpsing God's Heart

A. Read John 19:19–22.

1. Who authored the notice that was fastened to the cross?

2. What did this notice say?

3. What languages were used to convey the message of the notice? Why these three?

4. How did the chief priests react to the notice? Why?

5. How did Pilate respond to the chief priests? Why?

B. Read Luke 23:38–43.

1. How did one of the criminals crucified with Jesus relate to him? Why?

2. How did the other criminal respond to Jesus? Why?

3. How does verse 42 show that the second criminal may have been influenced by the sign on Jesus' cross?

4. How did Jesus respond to the request of this second criminal?

C. Read Romans 10:17.

1. How does faith come to an individual?

2. What is meant by "the word of Christ" (NIV)?

3. How would you lead someone to faith in Christ, according to this verse? If you have ever had this privilege, describe what happened.

D. Read 1 Corinthians 9:22.

1. What methods did the apostle Paul use to preach Christ to others?

2. What does this verse teach us about using the right "languages" to reach men and women for Christ?

3. What did Paul mean by "all possible means" (NIV)? What does this suggest to us about our evangelistic efforts?

Making a Choice

A. Make a list of ten persons you know who have not yet accepted Christ into their heart. Begin praying this week that God would give some believer—especially you—an open door to introduce each person to Jesus. Then start looking for opportunities to testify to your friends about the love of Christ.

B. Do a brief survey of the Book of Acts to see what methods and occasions the apostles used to preach Christ to unsaved men and women. What methods did they use? What sort of "languages" did God use to bring people to himself in the Book of Acts?

6

"I Will Let You Choose"

Nailing It Down

A. "Edwin and James Booth. Same father, mother, profession, and passion—yet one chooses life, the other, death. How could it happen? I don't know, but it does."

1. What could explain why these two brothers made such different choices?

2. What factors most influence the choices you make? Desire for security? Love? Fear? Conscience? Sense of right and wrong?

B. "In every age of history, on every page of Scripture, the truth is revealed: God allows us to make our own choices."

1. Why do you think God allows us to make our own choices?

2. What "big" choices are facing you right now? How will you make them?

C. "God gives eternal choices, and these choices have eternal consequences."

1. What does Max mean by "eternal choices"?

2. Is it fair that some choices have eternal consequences? Explain.

D. "There are times when God sends thunder to stir us. There are times when God sends blessings to lure us. But then there are times when God sends nothing but silence as he honors us with the freedom to choose where we spend eternity."
   1. Describe a time when God sent thunder to stir you.

   2. Has God ever sent blessings to lure you? Explain.

   3. Why would God be silent when we're faced with such a huge choice?

E. "The thief who repented is enjoying the fruit of the one good choice he made. In the end all his bad choices were redeemed by a solitary good one."
   1. Is it fair that all of one's bad choices can be redeemed by a single good one? Explain.

   2. Do you know someone who, toward the end of his life, made a decision for Christ? Describe that person's conversion.

Glimpsing God's Heart

A. Read Matthew 27:38–44 and Luke 23:39–43.
   1. What kind of men were crucified with Jesus? Describe them.

2. How do we know that a change occurred in the heart of one of these two men? What do you think brought about this change?

3. How did Jesus respond to this man's request? Why did he respond like this?

B. Read Colossians 1:12–14.
1. Who took the initiative in this passage? What did he do?

2. In what are we to "share"? How was this made possible?

3. From what were we rescued? To what were we delivered?

4. What have we been given in "the Son he loves" (NIV)?

C. Read Matthew 6:24; 7:13–14, 24–27; 25:32–33.
1. What choices are we given in each of these passages?

2. What choices have you made in each of these areas of life? How did you make these choices?

D. Read Deuteronomy 30:19–20 and Joshua 24:14–15.
1. What choices are presented in these passages? Who is to do the choosing?

2. What choice have you made in this crucial area of life? Explain.

Making a Choice

A. Read a biography of a celebrated Christian hero of the past, and pay particular attention to the hard choices he or she made. What prompted these choices? What might have happened had he or she refused to make the hard choice? How can you benefit from his or her example?

B. If you have already made the choice to receive Jesus Christ as your Savior and Lord, journal your testimony, focusing on how you came to that choice. Then spend some time pondering what God did to win your heart.

7

"I Will Not Abandon You"

Nailing It Down

A. "Just look at Mom's face as she nurses her baby. Just watch Dad's eyes as he cradles the child. And just try to harm or speak evil of the infant. If you do, you'll encounter a mighty strength, for the love of a parent is a mighty force."

   1. Describe an incident in which you or someone you know has displayed this "mighty force" Max talks about.

   2. Can you explain why the love of a parent is such a potent force?

B. "If we humans who are sinful have such a love, how much more does God, the sinless and selfless Father, love us? But what happens when the love isn't returned? What happens to the heart of the father when his child turns away?"

   1. How have you experienced the love of God? How has he expressed his Fatherly love to you?

   2. How did your parents react when one of their children rebelled? If you have children, how do you react? How do you think God reacts?

C. "Pride says, 'You're too good for him.' Shame says, 'You're too bad for him.' Pride drives you away. Shame keeps you away. If pride is what goes before a fall, then shame is what keeps you from getting up after one."

1. How are pride and shame connected? What similarities do they share?

2. To which are you more susceptible, pride or shame? Explain.

D. "Madeline swallowed hard and looked at the envelope. She opened it and removed the card. 'I know where you are,' it read. 'I know what you do. This doesn't change the way I feel. What I've said in each letter is still true.'"

1. Try to put yourself in Madeline's shoes. What would have kept you from reading your father's letters? What finally would cause you to read them?

2. Try to put yourself in the father's shoes. How would you feel when you discovered your daughter's situation? Why wouldn't it change the way you felt toward her?

E. "Will you come home and dance with your poppa again?"

1. Describe your feelings when you first read this line.

2. Has God ever asked you to "come home and dance" with him again? If so, describe the situation.

Glimpsing God's Heart

A. Read Luke 15:11–24.

1. What caused the young man to leave his home?

2. What happened to him after he left home?

3. How did he react when he ran out of money? What was his plan?

4. How did the father react to his son's return? What part of the young man's speech did the father not allow him to recite?

5. Why did the father react like this? How is this a picture of God?

B. Read Romans 5:6–11.

1. When did Christ die for "the ungodly" (NIV)? Who is included among "the ungodly"?

2. What contrast does this passage use to magnify the love of God? What is so unusual about it?

3. What does it mean to be "justified by his blood" (NIV)?

4. What does it mean to be "saved from God's wrath" (NIV) through Jesus?

5. What is the connection between being "reconciled" and being "saved"? How are they to be distinguished from one another?

6. What should be our response to being reconciled to God?

C. Read 2 Corinthians 5:19.

1. How did God reconcile sinners to himself?

2. Why doesn't God count any sins against those who have been reconciled?

3. How does one become reconciled to God? Why isn't it just automatic?

Making a Choice

A. Compare and contrast the story of the prodigal son in Luke 15 with the tragic story of David and Absalom in 2 Samuel 13–19:8. In what ways are these stories similar? In what ways are they different? What might David have done to avoid the tragedy that befell his family?

B. If you have children, think of something special to do with them to show your unconditional love for each of them. Maybe it's writing a long letter; maybe it's a special date "out on the town"; maybe it's a trip where your son or daughter is the center of attention. Whatever it is, plan it and carry it out as soon as possible.

8

"I Will Give You My Robe"

Nailing It Down

A. "I needed a jacket, but all I had was a prayer. The fellow was too kind to turn me away but too loyal to lower the standard. So the very one who required a jacket gave me a jacket, and we were given a table. Isn't this what happened at the cross?"

1. How is Max's story like what happened at the cross?

2. How is Max's story unlike what happened at the cross?

B. "Garments can symbolize character, and like his garment, Jesus' character was seamless. Coordinated. Unified. He was like his robe: uninterrupted perfection."

1. In what way was Jesus' character "seamless"?

2. Why was it crucial that Jesus' character be seamless?

C. "When Christ was nailed to the cross, he took off his robe of seamless perfection and assumed a different wardrobe, the wardrobe of indignity."

1. How did Jesus experience the following indignities?
    - the indignity of nakedness
    - the indignity of failure
    - the indignity of sin

2. Put yourself at the scene of the cross. As a follower of Jesus, which of these indignities would be hardest for you to see him endure? Why?

D. "While on the cross, Jesus felt the indignity and disgrace of a criminal. No, he was not guilty. No, he had not committed a sin. And, no, he did not deserve to be sentenced. But you and I were, we had, and we did."
   1. In what sense are you and I "criminals"?

   2. Why is it necessary to believe you really are a "criminal" before you can come to faith in Christ?

E. "Jesus offers a robe of seamless purity and dons my patchwork coat of pride, greed, and selfishness."
   1. How can we accept Jesus' offer of a robe of seamless purity? Have you done so? Explain.

   2. What are we to do with our "patchwork coat of pride, greed, and selfishness"? How in particular is this done?

Glimpsing God's Heart

A. Read John 19:23–24.
   1. What did the soldiers do with Jesus' clothes? Why did they do this?

   2. Why did the soldiers not tear Jesus' robe?

3. How did the soldiers unwittingly fulfill prophecy?

B. Read 1 Peter 2:24–25; 3:18; Galatians 3:13.

1. What did Jesus do with our sins, according to 1 Peter 2:24? What was the result?

2. What is the significance of the phrase "once for all" (NIV) in 1 Peter 3:18? Why is this crucial to remember? What was the purpose of his death?

3. How was the law a "curse" to us as described in Galatians 3:13? How was this curse removed? How was this, too, a fulfillment of prophecy?

C. Read Galatians 3:26–29 and Romans 13:8–14.

1. How does one become a child of God, according to Galatians 3:26? How does someone clothe himself with Christ (v. 27)? What does this mean?

2. What are the benefits of wearing such clothing, according to Galatians 3:29? What does this mean to you personally?

3. Why does Paul make a distinction between "our salvation" and "when we first believed" in Romans 13:11? How are the two related? How are they different from one another?

4. What does Paul mean by "clothe yourselves with the Lord Jesus Christ" in Romans 13:14? Does this differ from his use of the same metaphor in Galatians 3:27? Explain.

Making a Choice

A. What aspects of Christ's seamless character are most difficult for you to "put on"? What areas of life cause you the most struggles? How can you "clothe yourself with Christ" in those areas? Do an inventory of your life, and identify the three biggest challenges you face in the area of godly character development. Then spend some time taking these things to the Lord, asking him to help you "put on Christ" in these difficult areas.

B. Visit a rescue mission, homeless shelter, or benevolence ministry of a local church. Donate some time to feed the hungry or clean up around the place. Call ahead to see how you might contribute clothing or food for their use, and be sure to bring good quality items. Use your gift giving as an opportunity to remind yourself of the new spiritual clothes you wear because of Christ. And give thanks.

9

"I Invite You into My Presence"

Nailing It Down

A. "What did fifteen hundred years of a curtain-draped Holy of Holies communicate? Simple. God is holy . . . separate from us and unapproachable."

1. What does the word *holy* mean to you? How would you define it for someone who had never heard of the word?

2. Why is God intent on communicating his holiness to us? Why is this so vital?

B. "Jesus hasn't left us with an unapproachable God. Yes, God is holy. Yes, we are sinful. But, yes, yes, yes, Jesus is our mediator."

1. What is the function of a mediator? How is Jesus our mediator with God?

2. How has Jesus made God approachable? How often do you avail yourself of this free access to God?

C. "We are welcome to enter into God's presence—any day, any time. God has removed the barrier that separates us from him. The barrier of sin? Down. He has removed the curtain."

1. In what way are we not only *able* to enter God's presence but *welcome* there? What difference does this make?

2. What is this "curtain" that has been removed? How was it removed?

D. "We have a tendency to put the barrier back up. Though there is no curtain in a temple, there is a curtain in the heart. Like the ticks on the clock are the mistakes of the heart. And sometimes, no, oftentimes, we allow those mistakes to keep us from God. Our guilty conscience becomes a curtain that separates us from God."

1. Do you suffer from this tendency to "put the barrier back up"? If so, what usually causes you to put up a barrier?

2. How can you prevent guilt from erecting a curtain that separates you from God?

E. "Somewhere, sometime, somehow you got tangled up in garbage, and you've been avoiding God. You've allowed a veil of guilt to come between you and your Father. You wonder if you could ever feel close to God again. The message of the torn flesh is you can. God welcomes you. God is not avoiding you. God is not resisting you. The curtain is down, the door is open, and God invites you in."

1. Describe a time in your life when you tried to avoid God. How did you work through this crisis?

2. Is there a difference between *feeling* that the door to God is closed and that door actually *being* closed? Explain.

Glimpsing God's Heart

A. Read Leviticus 10:1–3; 16:1–2.

1. Why were Aaron's two sons killed in Leviticus 10? Who did the killing? What does this teach us?

2. What instructions did Aaron receive in Leviticus 16? What did this teach him (and us) about approaching God?

B. Read Matthew 27:50–51.

1. What happened when Jesus cried out for the final time?

2. What is significant about the phrase "from the top to the bottom"?

C. Read Ephesians 2:13–18.

1. According to verse 13, how were we brought near to God?

2. According to verses 15–16, how did Jesus break down the barrier?

3. According to verse 18, how do we have access to the Father?

D. Read 1 Timothy 2:5–6.

1. Who is the mediator between God and man? Is there more than one? Explain.

2. According to verse 6, what did Jesus do? What did he accomplish by this act?

E. Read Hebrews 10:19–22; 4:16.
   1. With what kind of attitude can we approach God, according to Hebrews 10:19? How is this possible?

   2. With what does Hebrews 10:20 compare Jesus' body? Why does it make this comparison?

   3. According to verse 22, how should we respond to Jesus' work on our behalf? What are we to do with a "guilty conscience"?

   4. According to Hebrews 4:16, how are we to approach God? Why are we to approach our Lord in prayer?

Making a Choice

A. Find a good book on prayer and commit yourself to reading it this month. Keep a journal as you read, and note in it the insights that especially speak to your heart.

B. If you're not already keeping a prayer journal, try it for one month. Get a little notebook, and in one column write down the date you prayed about a specific need. Keep the second column open to record when and how God answered your prayer.

10

"I Understand Your Pain"

Nailing It Down

A. "Why did Jesus live on the earth as long as he did? Couldn't his life have been much shorter? Why not step into our world just long enough to die for our sins and then leave? Why not a sinless year or week? Why did he have to live a life?"

1. Why do you think Jesus lived on the earth as long as he did?

2. If Jesus had been killed as an infant and raised to life three days later, what questions of ours might have gone unanswered? How would such an event have changed the nature of our faith?

B. "Before the nail was pounded, a drink was offered. Mark says the wine was mixed with myrrh. Matthew described it as wine mixed with gall. Both myrrh and gall contain sedative properties that numb the senses. But Jesus refused them. He refused to be stupefied by the drugs, opting instead to feel the full force of his suffering."

1. Why do you think Jesus refused to drink the sedatives?

2. Would you respond to Jesus differently if he had chosen to dull the pain? Explain.

C. "Jesus has been where you are and can relate to how you feel. And if his life on earth doesn't convince you, his death on the cross should. He understands what you are going through."

1. Do you ever feel as though Jesus just doesn't understand you or your circumstances? Explain.

2. How will our attitudes change if we really believe and understand that Jesus can relate to how we feel? How will it change our prayer life?

D. "Why did the throat of heaven grow raw? So we would know that he understands; so all who struggle would hear his invitation: 'You can trust me.'"

1. How does Jesus' parched throat show that we can trust him?

2. What does it mean to trust Jesus on a day-to-day basis?

E. "Why, in his final moments, was Jesus determined to fulfill prophecy? He knew we would doubt. He knew we would question. And since he did not want our heads to keep his love from our hearts, he used his final moments to offer proof that he was the Messiah."

1. How does fulfilled prophecy help us to trust God?

2. What fulfilled prophecies most help you to trust God?

Glimpsing God's Heart

A. Read Mark 15:22–24.

1. What did the Romans offer Jesus just before they crucified him?

2. How did Jesus respond? Why did he respond like this?

B. Read John 19:28–30.

1. How does this scene differ from the one in Mark 15?

2. How was this scene a fulfillment of prophecy? Why was it important to finish this work before his death?

C. Read Hebrews 4:15–16.

1. Why is Jesus called our "high priest"?

2. Why is Jesus able to sympathize with our weaknesses?

3. What one area of life did Jesus not share with us? Why is this crucial?

D. Read 2 Corinthians 1:3–5.

1. What is God called in verse 3?

2. Why does God comfort us, according to verse 4?

3. How are our sufferings and comfort related, according to verse 5?

Making a Choice

A. Take several weeks to thoroughly read the four Gospels. Keep a notebook by your Bible, and record every instance in which Jesus demonstrates his deep understanding of human weaknesses and troubles.

B. Be on the lookout this week for ways you can convey Christ's compassion to others. Let your friends or coworkers see that you understand and appreciate their unique troubles. Let your family know that you are trying your best to understand their personal challenges. Do something out of the ordinary, a special step out of your comfort zone.

11

"I Have Redeemed You and I Will Keep You"

Nailing It Down

A. "I get credit for the good work of someone else simply by virtue of being on his team. Hasn't Christ done the same for you? What my team did for me on Monday, your Lord does for you every day of the week. Because of his performance, you close your daily round with a perfect score."

1. Describe a time you got credit for being on a successful team.

2. What does it mean to you to be on "the Lord's team"?

B. "Positional sanctification comes because of Christ's work *for* us. Progressive sanctification comes because of Christ's work *in* us. Both are gifts from God."

1. In your own words, describe what "positional sanctification" means to you.

2. In your own words, describe what "progressive sanctification" means to you.

3. In what way are both of them God's gift to you?

C. "Marriage is both a done deal and a daily development, something you did and something you do. The same is true of our walk with God. Can you be more saved than you were the first day of your salvation? No. But can a person grow in salvation? Absolutely. It, like marriage, is a done deal and a daily development."

1. In what way is marriage a "done deal"? In what way is it a "daily development"?

2. How is your walk with God like a marriage? How is it different?

D. "Some accept the blood but forget the water. They want to be saved but don't want to be changed. Others accept the water but forget the blood. They are busy for Christ but never at peace in Christ. What about you? Do you tend to lean one way or the other?"

1. Answer Max's question. Which way do you tend to lean?

2. How can someone who is saved mature in the faith so that he or she *wants* to be changed?

3. How can someone who is frantically busy for Christ also find peace in Christ?

Glimpsing God's Heart

A. Read John 19:31–37.

1. Why were the legs of the two criminals broken? Why were Jesus' legs not broken?

2. Why do you think the soldier pierced Jesus' side? What happened when he did?

3. In verse 35 John says he relates the information about Jesus' pierced side so that "you also may believe" (NIV). What does he mean?

B. Read John 7:37–39.
1. What promise does Jesus give us in this passage?

2. In what way is the Spirit like a stream of living water? What must we do to avail ourselves of this water?

C. Read Hebrews 9:11–12.
1. How was Jesus able to enter the heavenly Most Holy Place?

2. What kind of redemption did Jesus win for us?

D. Read Hebrews 10:10, 12, 14.
1. How have we been made holy according to verse 10?

2. According to verse 12, how many sacrifices did Jesus make? For how long was this sacrifice to remain effective?

3. What two tenses appear in verse 14? What is significant about this? How is it possible to both be "made perfect forever" while "being made holy"?

E. Read Philippians 2:12–13.
   1. What does it mean to "work out your salvation" (NIV)?
   2. Why are we to do this with "fear and trembling"?
   3. Who is at work in us? What is he up to?

Making a Choice

A. Approach your spouse or best friend in the Lord and ask him or her to tell you where you seem strongest spiritually: (1) in your confidence as a child of God, or (2) in your work as a servant of the King. Gently probe the reasons for their answer. Then take this evaluation and bring it before the Lord in prayer, asking him to help you grow and mature in the area where you're weaker.

B. Get out an exhaustive concordance like the *NIV Exhaustive Concordance,* and do a word study on the term *sanctify* (as well as *sanctifying*). What do you learn? What part is God's responsibility, and what part is our responsibility? How does this change the way you approach spiritual growth?

12

"I Will Love You Forever"

Nailing It Down

A. "How can God be both just and kind? How can he dispense truth and mercy? How can he redeem the sinner without endorsing the sin? Can a holy God overlook our mistakes? Can a kind God punish our mistakes? From our perspective there are only two equally unappealing solutions. But from his perspective there is a third. It's called 'the Cross of Christ.'"

1. Answer Max's five questions above.

2. How is the Cross of Christ God's solution to our dilemma?

B. "The cross is where God forgave his children without lowering his standards. How could he do this? In a sentence: God put our sin on his Son and punished it there."

1. How does the cross show both God's holiness and his love?

2. How did God put our sin on his Son? What is required for his Son's merit to be charged to our account?

C. "Surely there has to be an end to God's love. You'd think so, wouldn't you? But David the adulterer never found it. Paul the murderer never found it. Peter the liar never found it. When it came to life, they hit bottom. But when it came to God's love, they never did."

1. Describe a time when you thought you had reached the end of God's love for you. What happened?

2. How can you help others to understand and even feel the limitless depth of God's love?

Glimpsing God's Heart

A. Read John 3:16–18.

1. According to this passage, who may gain eternal life? How is this done?

2. Why did God send his Son to earth, according to verse 16?

3. What *didn't* God send his Son to earth to do, according to verse 17?

4. Who is not condemned, according to verse 18? Who is condemned, according to the same verse? To which group do you belong? Explain.

B. Read 2 Corinthians 5:21.

1. What did God do with his Son?
2. For whom did he do this?
3. Why did he do this?

C. Read Romans 5:8.
    1. How did God demonstrate his love for us?

    2. When did God demonstrate this love? Why is that utterly remarkable?

D. Read 1 John 4:10.
    1. Where does real love begin?

    2. Why did God send his Son? What is "an atoning sacrifice" (NIV)?

E. Read Romans 11:22.
    1. What two "sides" of God are described in this verse?

    2. What practical application does the apostle Paul make from this truth?

Making a Choice

A. Sometimes a famous verse can become so familiar that it loses some of its punch. John 3:16 may well fit into that category. To help yourself feel the surging power of this verse, look it up in several translations. Write the verse as it appears in each of these versions. Then spend some time pondering how they all communicate the same glorious truth. Conclude your time by spending several minutes in prayer, thanking God for sending Christ to earth *for you*.

B. The next time you're watching a sporting event on television and you get a glimpse of the "John 3:16 guy" (he attends a lot of games!), ask whoever is in the room why he or she thinks the guy insists on appearing with his sign at so many events. Try to start a discussion about the meaning behind the verse.

13

"I Can Turn Your Tragedy into Triumph"

Nailing It Down

A. "On the first Easter Sunday, God took clothing of death and made it a symbol of life. Could he do the same for you?"

1. What clothing of death did God make into a symbol of life?

2. Answer Max's question. Could God do something similar for you? Explain.

B. "When it's Saturday in your life, how do you react? When you are somewhere between yesterday's tragedy and tomorrow's triumph, what do you do? Do you leave God—or do you linger near him?"

1. What does Max mean by "Saturday in your life"?

2. Answer Max's question. After tragedy strikes, do you leave God or linger near him? Explain.

C. "Through the rags of death, John saw the power of life. Odd, don't you think, that God would use something as sad as a burial wrap to change a life?"

1. Do you think it's odd that God would use a burial wrap to change a life? Explain.

2. Discuss some other biblical instances where God took a sad thing and made it into a glad thing.

D. "As hard as it may be to believe, you could be only a Saturday away from a resurrection. You could be only hours from that precious prayer of a changed heart, 'God, did you do this for me?'"
   1. What kind of "resurrection" do you need right now?
   2. Do you believe God is willing to give you this resurrection, just for you? Explain.

Glimpsing God's Heart

A. Read John 19:38–40; 20:3–9.
   1. Who came to take down the body of Jesus? What did these men have in common? How did they display more courage at this hour than any of Jesus' disciples?
   2. How did these men prepare Jesus' body for burial? How does this prove that Jesus was really and truly dead?
   3. What did Peter and "the other disciple" (John, NIV) find when they entered the empty tomb on the day of Jesus' resurrection (John 20:5–7)? Why did what they saw cause John to believe?

B. Read Psalm 31:7–8.
   1. Why was the psalmist glad? Name at least three reasons.
   2. How can this text encourage us in tough times?

C. Read 1 Peter 5:10.

1. What title is God given in this verse? How is it significant?

2. To what did God call us?

3. When will we be "restored" and be made "strong, firm and steadfast" (NIV)?

D. Read Romans 8:28.

1. What does this verse say we "know"?

2. What is significant about the phrase "in all things" or "in everything"?

3. To whom is this promise given? What are the two "requirements"?

4. How can this verse give us hope in difficult times?

Making a Choice

A. Follow through on Max's suggestion: "Do this simple exercise. Remove the word *everything* [in Romans 8:28], and replace it with the symbol of your tragedy." What happens when you do this?

B. On your own or with someone else, think of several stories in the Bible in which God took what appeared to be a clear defeat for his people and turned it into a triumph. Why do you think God so enjoys doing things this way? In what area of your life could you use such a triumph right now? Enlist a friend to pray with you that God would engineer just such a reversal on your behalf.

14

"I Have Won the Victory"

Nailing It Down

A. What statement in each of the five sections in this chapter helped you the most?

1. His Birth
2. His Ministry
3. His Execution
4. His Movement
5. The Movement Continues

B. What statement startled you the most? Why?

Glimpsing God's Heart

A. Read Colossians 2:15.

1. How did God turn the cross from an object of shame into an object of exaltation?
2. How did God turn the cross from an object of death into an object of life?
3. How did God turn the cross from an object of horror into an object of joy?

4. How did the cross give God his greatest victory over Satan?

5. Do you think Satan saw his defeat coming? Explain.

B. Read 1 Corinthians 15:57 as quoted at the beginning of the chapter.
   1. What three enemies were conquered at the cross?

   2. How was this made possible?

   3. Who made this possible?

   4. What is to be our response to this glorious victory?

C. Read 2 Corinthians 2:14.
   1. What are we promised in this verse?

   2. What kind of "victories" are in view?

   3. How is the cross an example of these victories?

   4. What does the reality of the cross suggest about the appearance of our own spiritual victories?

Making a Choice

A. Even if you're far from being a poet, try to compose a few lines of poetry that describe your feelings about Christ's empty tomb. Emphasize what is most meaningful to you.

Then, if you're brave enough, show what you've written to a kind and gentle friend. (Or simply make a list of words that convey your feelings about Christ's victory over death.)

B. Imagine that you were one of the angels assigned to the tomb after Jesus' resurrection—maybe the one who rolled away the stone and sat on it, the one who caused the soldiers guarding the tomb to faint dead away with uncontrollable fright. What would go through your mind? What emotions would you feel? What would you want to do? Whom would you want to speak to? What would you say to Jesus after he rose from the dead? If you had been the first one to see him alive after his resurrection, how would you have greeted him?

15

What Will You Leave at the Cross?

Nailing It Down

A. "Absurdities and ironies. The hill of Calvary is nothing if not both."

1. What absurdities surround the hill of Calvary?

2. What ironies surround the hill of Calvary?

3. Which intrigue you the most, the absurdities or the ironies? Why?

B. "We wouldn't have written the drama of redemption this way. But, then again, we weren't asked to. These players and props were heaven picked and God ordained. We were not asked to design the hour. But we have been asked to respond to it. In order for the cross of Christ to be the cross of your life, you and I need to bring something to the hill."

1. How would you have written the drama of redemption, had you been asked to be its author?

2. How have you responded to Calvary?

3. What have you brought to the hill?

C. Max urges us to leave something at the cross. In each of the following categories, what can you leave at Calvary?

1. Bad moments

2. Mad moments

3. Anxious moments

4. Final moment

Glimpsing God's Heart

A. Read John 14:1–3.
   1. What was troubling Jesus' disciples at the time he spoke these words?

   2. What counsel did he give them to relieve their worries?

   3. How is this counsel equally applicable to us today?

B. Read 1 John 1:9.
   1. What promise is given to us in this verse?

   2. What confession do you need to leave at Calvary?

C. Read 1 Corinthians 13:5.
   1. What characteristics does love *not* have, according to this verse?

   2. Which of these sins is Christ asking you to leave at Calvary?

D. Read Proverbs 3:5–6.
   1. What are we instructed to do in these verses?
   2. How is this to be done, practically speaking?
   3. What promise does this verse give us?
   4. What do you have to leave at the cross in order to benefit from the promise of this verse?

E. Read 1 Peter 5:7.
   1. What are we instructed to do in this verse?
   2. What promise is given to those who obey this instruction?
   3. What do you have to leave at the cross in order to benefit from the promise of this verse?

Making a Choice

A. As much as possible, make a list of all your bad moments, mad moments, and anxious moments. Confess them to the Lord, then take your list to some remote place and there shred it and bury it at the foot of a tree. On your way home, thank the Lord that he invites you to place all of these troubling things at the foot of the cross—the only place they can be drained of their power.

B. Plan and carry out a personal worship service to which you invite only family members (or no one else at all). Carefully pick out several hymns or choruses or songs that help you to focus on all the amazing things God did to win your heart, and sing them with abandon. Read several short portions of Scripture that remind you of the lengths to which he went for you. Spend several minutes thanking him for his grace . . . and for the nails that fastened Christ (and your sins) to the cross. Have a great, joyful time—and bring joy to the heart of God through your outpouring of praise.

INSPIRATIONAL BOOKS FROM MAX LUCADO

WHEN CHRIST COMES

Wouldn't it be refreshing to discuss the end of time and feel better because of it? Or to hear some truly comforting words regarding the return of Christ? As only master storyteller Max Lucado can do, he takes readers on an unforgettable journey to show what will happen on the glorious day *When Christ Comes*.

JUST LIKE JESUS

"What if, for one day, Jesus became you," asks master storyteller Max Lucado. With this simple premise, Lucado tells how God loves you just the way you are, but he refuses to leave you that way. He wants you to be . . . *Just Like Jesus*.

THE GREAT HOUSE OF GOD

God's greatest desire is to be your dwelling place—the home for your heart. Warm your heart by the fire in the living room. Nourish your spirit in the kitchen. Step into the hallway and find forgiveness. No house is more complete, no foundation more solid. So come into the house built just for you... *The Great House of God*.

In The Grip of Grace

In his most theologically challenging book yet, Max Lucado shows how you can't fall beyond God's love. "God doesn't condone our sin, nor does He compromise His standard. Rather than dismiss our sin, He assumes our sin and incredibly, incredibly sentences Himself. God is still holy. Sin is still sin. And we are redeemed."

A Gentle Thunder

How far do you want God to go in getting your attention? Don't answer too quickly. What if God moved you to another land? (as He did Abraham.) What if He called you out of retirement? (Remember Moses?) How about the voice of an angel or the bowel of a fish (Gideon and Jonah.) God does what it takes to get our attention. Softly shouting, gently thundering…whatever it takes to get us home safely.

When God Whispers Your Name

Perhaps you've never seen your name honored. And you can't remember when you heard it spoken with kindness. If you're struggling to find your way, Lucado offers the inspiration to believe that God has already bought the ticket—with your name on it. This book affirms that God can move you along on your journey with power from beyond.

HE STILL MOVES STONES

Why does the Bible contain so many stories of hurting people? Lucado reminds us that the purpose of these portraits isn't to tell us what Jesus did—but rather to remind us what Jesus still does. He comes to do what you can't. He comes to move the stones you can't budge. *He Still Moves Stones.*

THE APPLAUSE OF HEAVEN

It is what you always dreamed but never expected. It's having God as your dad, your biggest fan, and your best friend. It is having the King of kings in your cheering section. Max Lucado shows you how the Beatitudes provide what we need to discover the joy of God. Much more than a "how-to" book on happiness; *The Applause of Heaven* is an encounter with the Source of Joy.

IN THE EYE OF THE STORM

Come face-to-face with Jesus when He experienced more stress than any other day of his life aside from his crucifixion. With keen insight and exacting clarity, Max Lucado shows us the secret of transforming panic into peace, stress into serenity, and chaos into control.

COSMIC CHRISTMAS

Was the birth of Jesus a quietly profound event? Or could it have included heavenly battles, angel armies, and a scheming Satan? Come along as Lucado takes us on a journey into his imagination—pulling back the curtain as we see what might have taken place one *Cosmic Christmas.*

THE CHRISTMAS CROSS

The Christmas Cross is a story about finding your way home for the holidays, told in the context of one man's journey in a small Texas town. Unique interactive elements inside this book—including envelopes with pullout letters and surprises—make this a one-of-a-kind Christmas treasure.

THE INSPIRATIONAL BIBLE

Imagine studying the Bible with Max Lucado. He sees the Bible as "stories of real people, real problems, real joy, and a real Savior." Edited by Max Lucado, *The Inspirational Bible* includes:

- 700 "Life Lessons"
- Introductions to each book of the Bible
- 48 color pages that address topics from Forgiveness to Victory

MORE THAN A BOOK.

MORE THAN THE STORY OF THE CROSS.

MORE THAN YOU'VE EVER IMAGINED.

Join Max Lucado as he invites you to examine the cross, contemplate its purpose, and celebrate its significance with *He Chose the Nails.* If you've been blessed by this book, these companion products are also available:

- the first Max Lucado stand-alone workbook
- the first Max Lucado leader's guide
- the first Max Lucado video package
- the praise and worship CD from Here to Him Music